Praise for *Landscape without Gravity*

"Like most worthwhile literature and art, *Landscape without Gravity* is a way of connecting with the human heart. . . . By cutting to the core of her own experience, Ascher has written a book about loss that is at once completely personal and universal. Her honesty touches the reader's heart, opens the scars of old wounds, and helps to heal them. . . . Wrenching. . . insightful . . . compelling."   —*The Boston Globe*

"Searing and poignant"
                              —*The New York Times*

"Poignant . . . engrossing and very moving . . . sparked with wit"
                              —*People*

"The book went straight to my heart in a few pages. It's a lovely book and an immensely brave one. *Landscape without Gravity* describes the journey through grief's labyrinth more closely and movingly than anything else on the subject. What an admirable and hard-won balance between mourning and affirmation."
                              —Cyra McFadden, author of *Rain or Shine*

"A harrowing portrayal of grief"
                              —*New York Newsday*

"Lyrical . . . unflinching . . . marked by candor, humor, vivid imagery, and a spirit of affirmation"
                              —*Publishers Weekly*

"Powerful and profound . . . it is one of a kind, not only a work of art but a service to mankind. . . . Grief emanates like a vapor from the pages. The reader is caught up at once and held fast until the last word."   —Richard Selzer, author of *Raising the Dead*

PENGUIN BOOKS
LANDSCAPE WITHOUT GRAVITY

Barbara Lazear Ascher is the author of *Playing After Dark* (1986) and *The Habit of Loving* (1989). She lives with her husband in New York City.

LANDSCAPE
WITHOUT
GRAVITY
A MEMOIR OF GRIEF

BARBARA
LAZEAR
ASCHER

PENGUIN BOOKS

PENGUIN BOOKS
Published by the Penguin Group
Penguin Books USA Inc., 375 Hudson Street,
New York, New York 10014, U.S.A.
Penguin Books Ltd, 27 Wrights Lane,
London W8 5TZ, England
Penguin Books Australia Ltd, Ringwood,
Victoria, Australia
Penguin Books Canada Ltd, 10 Alcorn Avenue,
Toronto, Ontario, Canada M4V 3B2
Penguin Books (N.Z.) Ltd, 182–190 Wairau Road,
Auckland 10, New Zealand

Penguin Books Ltd, Registered Offices:
Harmondsworth, Middlesex, England

First published in the United States of America by Delphinium Books Inc., 1993
Published in Penguin Books 1994

10 9 8 7 6 5 4 3 2 1

The excerpt from the poetry of Wallace Stevens on page 53 is from *Collected Poems* by Wallace Stevens. Copyright © 1923 and renewed © 1951 by Wallace Stevens. Reprinted by permission of Alfred A. Knopf, Inc.

The excerpt from T. S. Eliot's poem "East Coker" on page 155 is from *Four Quartets*, copyright © 1943 by T. S. Eliot and renewed © 1971 by Esme Valerie Eliot. Reprinted by permission of Harcourt Brace Jovanovich, Inc.

THE LIBRARY OF CONGRESS HAS CATALOGUED THE HARDCOVER AS FOLLOWS:
Ascher, Barbara Lazear.
Landscape without gravity: a memoir of grief/Barbara Lazear Ascher.
p.   cm.
ISBN 0-671-79676-3 (hc.)
ISBN 0 14 02.3495 0 (pbk.)
1. Grief—Case studies.   2. Brothers and sisters—United States—Death—Psychological aspects—Case studies.   3. AIDS (Disease)—Patients—United States—Death—Psychological aspects—Case studies.   4. Gay men—United States—Death—Psychological aspects—Case studies.   5. Lazear, Bobby—Death and burial.   6. Ascher, Barbara Lazear.   I. Title.
BF575.G7A78   1993
155.9′37—dc20   92–28088

Printed in the United States of America
Set in Helvetica
Designed by Milton Charles

This book is dedicated to
my sister, Rebecca Lazear Okrent,
to our parents, Robert Allen and
Dorothy Rector Lazear,
and to the memory of their son,
our brother, Robert Allen Lazear, Jr.

CONTENTS

"We feel close to each other when we see ourselves as strangers and outsiders on this planet or see the planet as an island of life in a dark immensity of nothingness. We also draw together when we are aware that night must close in on all living things; that we are condemned to death at birth; and that life is a bus ride to the place of execution. All our squabbling and vying are about seats in the bus, and the ride is over before we know it."
—Eric Hoffer, *In Our Time*

"Give sorrow words: the grief that does not speak
Whispers the o'er-fraught heart,
And bids it break."
—Shakespeare, *Macbeth*

INTRODUCTION

Until Bobby, my thirty-one-year-old brother, died I knew little of grief. I knew nothing of its might. I did not know that it is unpredictable, with a life of its own. I hadn't known that rage, guilt and remorse are sorrow's companions. I was unprepared for grief that extends beyond immediate loss to all loss remembered and anticipated.

As we flounder in this mystery, it is little wonder that those outside our grief urge us to "snap out of it," to "return to normal life." How are they to know that returning to normal life is a hero's journey through storm-tossed seas? We could lose our way. We could drown. We could drift for the rest of our days.

The journey that I have logged is not necessarily the journey of another, for grief is intensely individual. And although each member of my family shared the same loss, the privacy of their grief is not mine to invade.

Similarly, my observations of the family are not to be mistaken for "the truth." There is no single truth about a family anymore than there is about grief. We bring ourselves to these events. What is individual response is not to be confused with a static "reality."

Grief is a solo, often silent journey, but we draw together as we pause to stare into the void and struggle to give sorrow words. These are mine.

LANDSCAPE
WITHOUT
GRAVITY
A MEMOIR OF GRIEF

PROLOGUE

It could have been a parade of Civil War soldiers, wounded and near defeat, marching toward another battle. They stared ahead with eyes from which all joy had been banished.

They had marched in too many funeral processions, they had watched as disease dismissed courage and defiantly claimed their friends. This day they marched in a New Orleans jazz funeral for my brother, Bobby, dead of AIDS at thirty-one.

I rode with my sister, mother, father and my brother's companion, George, in a mule-drawn wagon, ahead of the parade of friends, and behind the musicians, old black men who knew the route and the music by heart.

The street was closed for the occasion. The citizens were shuttered inside cool interiors away from the fireball that is New Orleans' summer sun. The day was ours, the streets were ours. The sun beat down on us alone. We in the cart sat still as stones.

George cradled a carved wooden box that looked like an ornate bird house—the house of ashes that had been my brother's bones.

Still as stone we rode through the streets of New Orleans as jazz rose up around us and the band played "The Old Rugged Cross" to lead us to the church. If we moved, if we cried, we might never stop moving, never stop crying. It was better to be still.

My brother was a wild thing. The confines of our New England homes could not contain him. He kept flying into windows. Released, he flew south to warmth, to a landscape large enough to absorb his exuberance. To sympathetic souls who held him when exuberance failed.

A friend who volunteers at the Gay Men's Health Crisis told me in the early days of Bobby's illness when I called him for help, "You would be surprised how many families first learn that their son or brother is gay at the same time they learn he has AIDS. They get a phone call that starts, 'I've got two things to tell you.'" My family was more fortunate. Bobby's openness had enabled my parents to share the happiness he and George were finding together, to know and accept that in a careless world, love is precious whatever the pairing. But there is no accepting that one's child is doomed.

We are not alone in our anger, grief, and disbelief. The horizon fills with parents burying their young. Fewer and fewer of us are allowed the smug certainty that AIDS has nothing to do with our lives. Soon, each of us will have a child, brother, friend, friend of a friend, a distant relative who is doomed.

For awhile the statistics insulated many of us. We read that the risk group comprised homosexuals, bisexuals and intravenous drug users. If we didn't fit in the categories, we said, "Well, I'm safe," and turned the page. To number fatalities is to depersonalize them. The body count in Vietnam. The deaths from drunk driving. Numbers don't touch our hearts.

My parents, well known in their community, broke through those barriers of denial by making it clear, in their son's prominent obituary, that the cause of Bobby's death was AIDS. Not "pneumonia" or "heart attack" or "respiratory failure," or other causes of death we see in obituary columns when we read about young men dying in their prime.

The letters of sympathy began to come in immediately.

"Thank you for being honest about Bobby's illness. My best friend's son has AIDS."

"When my cousin died of AIDS, it was a family secret, and that robbed us of the opportunity to mourn and be supported in our grief."

"My best friend in college, captain of the football team, a Rhodes scholar, just died of AIDS."

"My child got AIDS from a blood transfusion. We are afraid that she will be expelled from school if the truth is known. We are so alone in our mourning."

AIDS has come home. AIDS has come to Donna Reed America, to Father Knows Best America. AIDS kills kids who once wore Mickey Mouse Club caps and wrote mash notes to Annette Funicello.

When my sister and I first learned of Bobby's illness it seemed incomprehensible that this could be happening to our baby brother, that boy so blond and boisterous, that man so handsome, funny, smart and exasperating. We began a journey into paralysis. There were days when it seemed we had to concentrate on putting one foot in front of the other if we were to walk at all. If we traveled more than a couple of blocks, we were exhausted for the rest of the day.

We were hungry, we weren't hungry. We made chocolate chip cookies and chocolate brownies and didn't eat them. We opened and closed the refrigerator door, looking for something that might cushion the pain, fill the chasm that was opening from within.

Now I realize that this was the beginning of grief which starts in the stomach, yawning like the gaping mouth in Munch's painting, *The Scream.* But what did we know of grief? We were young, our beloveds had not yet died. I began to understand that grieving is like walking. The urge is there, but you need a guiding hand, you need someone to teach you how.

I was to learn that the death of a sibling, grievous in itself, is also a startling reminder of our own mortality. When a sibling dies, the absolute certainty of death replaces the cherished illusion that maybe we'll be the exceptions. When a sibling dies, death tugs at our own shirttails. There's no unclasping its persistent grip. "You too," it says. "Yes, even you."

When you are new to grief, you learn that there's no second-guessing it. It will have its way with you. Don't be fooled by the statistics you read: Widows have one bad year; orphans three. Grief doesn't read time tables.

One morning, three weeks after Bobby died, I arose feeling happy and energetic. Well, now, I thought, I guess we've taken care of that. Wrong. The next morning I was awakened by a wail I thought was coming from the storm outside until I realized it was coming from me.

Grief will fool you with its disguises. Some days you insist that you're fine, you're just angry at a friend who said the wrong thing at the wrong time. One day I wept into the lettuce and peaches at our local market when an acquaintance approached to scold me for my stand in an old battle. Of course, we both assumed that she was responsible for my tears.

Months after Bobby's death, my mother wept as she prepared breakfast. When my father asked, "Are you all right?" she said, "Yes, of course. I always cry when I poach eggs."

You learn that you can cry and stop and laugh and even follow a taxi driver's command to "Have a nice day," and then cry again. You learn that there is no such thing as crying forever. There was a time when I was certain that I would never be happy again. I was wrong.

Grief is like the wind. When it's blowing hard, you adjust your sails and run before it. If it blows too hard, you stay in the harbor, close the hatches and don't take calls. When it's gentle, you go sailing, have a picnic, take a swim.

You go wherever it takes you. There are no bulwarks to withstand it. Should you erect one, it will eventually tire of the game and blow the walls in.

We cannot know another's grief, as deeply personal as love and pain. I cannot measure my own against the sorrow of my sister, parents, or my brother's friends who must wonder every day who among them will be next. Who must have wondered, as they marched through the streets of New Orleans, which of their families would sit one day in the mule-drawn cart. I shy away from the magnitude of my brother's own grief when, upon being diagnosed, he heard the final click of the door closing on possibility.

A friend of mine said of her son when he died at thirty, "He was just beginning to look out at the world and make maps." So was my brother. And then there was no place to go.

CHAPTER I

EARTHQUAKE

"For the thing that I fear comes upon me,
and what I dread befalls me."—Job

EARTHQUAKE

Last night there was a roar that shook the earth. I reached for my husband's hand. "Bob!" I whispered. "Listen! Listen!" The little house in which we slept was perched on the shore of Sir Francis Drake Channel in the British Virgin Islands. It answered the roar with its own deep moan, a shifting of shingle and stone. The earth beneath us rocked like the sea. I thought we were afloat. I thought our foundations were opening like a yawn. I thought the world was coming to an end.

Deep within the earth's bowels there was a colliding, exploding, chaotic tumble of rock. I stared up at the ceiling waiting for it to fall, and should it, I knew I would be unable to leap to my feet to save myself. Then there was stillness, as sudden and astounding as the shock preceding it. Even ordinary nocturnal sounds were silenced. Gone was the ripple of surf breaking on the reef. Gone, the soft rustle of tropical breezes in marsh grass. Gone were the songs and complaints of night creatures.

"Will there be a tidal wave?" I asked my husband who knows about such things. Ask him anything about water and he'll have the answer. "No." We awaited the aftershock, our silence matching the night's. All living things seemed to hold their breaths.

Once confident that the stillness was secure, I climbed from bed, and testing the steadiness of cool tiles beneath my feet, walked out onto the terrace. I was surprised to find the stars in their places. There was Betelgeuse above Tortola, and Regulus and Spica over Great Dog Island. They were like polite dinner guests who remain seated, making small talk in spite of the terrible fight that has ensued between host and hostess at the other end of the table.

It is always sobering to witness the cool remove of stars when you consider the heated prayers and wishes we send in their direction. It's as though we've been talking to their backs.

I returned to bed, but left-over fear and a sense that it would be irreverent to ignore what had happened kept me awake for the rest of the night. Gratitude welled up out of fear. Death had seemed so close and we'd been spared.

I understood why the ancients believed that such tumult in the earth's crust was the act of angry gods. That a groan emitted from the depths, growing louder until its volume seemed to cause the earth to rock and sway was a complaint from another world, rising from another consciousness. I understood a preference for a god, even a vicious god who took it all personally, to this random chaos.

When dawn dispelled nightmares and terror, it revealed an earth unscathed. I had expected to find jagged cracks in the soil, birds stunned on their perches, boulders tossed from hillside to beach. Instead, here was a morning like yesterday's and the day before that. The green hills received the rising sun's shower of gold, and large pink clouds were washed white by approaching light. It was clear that no notice had been taken.

I walked to the dining pavilion where other guests at the resort would be gathering for steaming coffee and cool mangoes. They would share their fears of the night and verify for me that the world had seemed, for a moment, to be on the brink of eternal damnation. I wanted to hear that others had been rocked to their souls. But the only sounds were the clinks of coffee cups meeting their saucers.

This was how it had been eight months earlier when Bobby was diagnosed as having AIDS.

As stunning as the soul-rocking shock of that event was the fact that the earth remained unchanged. Brueghel's plowman stared into his furrows as Icarus fell from heaven to the sea. Through May and June as I sat by the phone to receive the dismal medical reports, children continued to play outside my windows. They flew their kites, tossed their jacks and squabbled with each other. On street corners citizens waved their arms, hailing cabs as though daily life were an emergency. Con Ed, the butcher, the landlord sent their bills and expected me to pay. The doorbell rang and I was to answer. Friends awaited friendship in return. It was business as usual. The business of living. I watched and waited for some sign that my life had been changed forever. But there were no manifestations, no obvious cracks in my skull.

In mid-July my husband and I sailed for Nantucket to put distance between ourselves, the heat of Manhattan and the persistent sadness of impending loss. To have time alone to mourn that we had lost Bobby years ago and now had so little time to reach out and reconnect.

One hot morning as we were anchored in the harbor, as coffee was set to brew and the day's plans were being considered, the sound of engines drew close and there was a thump as another boat drew alongside our own. "Ahoy, *Barbie*!" We emerged from the cabin to see the local launch driver steadying himself against our gunwales. "Call your daughter!" he shouted, returned to the helm and was gone.

Dread took hold like a hand around the throat. Impending doom had left us vulnerable to the slightest noise in the night, to imagined horrors threatening beloveds we could not watch with our own eyes. Our magical guardian eyes.

Something terrible must have happened to our twenty-year-old daughter, Rebecca, or to her fiancée, Chuck, who were both at home in New York. I entertained a rush of possible calamities. Someone her age had recently been killed by a hit-and-run driver one block from our home. The previous year another had been murdered in Central Park. Whenever I left her behind it was with the awareness of the fragility of safety and now I had been proved correct.

Bob and I, both badly frightened by the sense of urgency in the message, coming as it had across water, made our call on the ship-to-shore radio rather than taking the time to row ashore to public phones. We gained time but sacrificed privacy, as a ship's radio broadcasts to all boats, serving as a nautical party line for those who want to tune in. When we reached Rebecca she cried, "I can't believe you're calling from the boat." My hands went cold. Something terrible had happened that she wanted to share with us alone, not the entire harbor. Something must have happened to Chuck.

"George called," she sobbed, gathered her breath and began again. "George called. Bobby died last night."

It had not occurred to me that the call might concern Bobby. He and I had spoken cheerfully and hopefully just before Bob and I left town. We planned to speak upon his return from an upcoming trip to the Virgin Islands. We promised each other a September reunion in New Orleans where George and he shared a home. He planned to come to New York in October or November and asked if I could get him theater tickets. I had believed in it.

Rebecca explained that she had called the Nantucket Coast Guard, which in turn had sent the launch driver out with the message. She wanted to know what to do next. My response was as it always is in crisis. A door opens and ice water pours forth, freezing me in place. I become cool and efficient. I look around to see who needs comforting, as though I can manage my own pain whereas others may not be able to manage theirs. I do not cry. I reached for the microphone and asked for the details. What time? Where? How could I reach George? My sister, Becky?

I gave orders and offered comfort. "I'm so sorry that you had to be the first to hear the news and to be the bearer of such terrible tidings," I told her. She was to call Becky's friends to find out where she and her husband and children were vacationing in California. They too were unprepared for disaster and had not left a forwarding address or phone number. My parents, on their little summer island, had no phone. All of us, believing that we had time, had gone about our normal lives. Now I realize that we were in the first stage of grief. We thought that by making independent plans we could slow death's insistent march.

"Good-bye, Rebecca. We'll call later this morning from the shore." And then the formalities, "Marine operator, this is sailing vessel *Barbie* signing off." "Thank you, *Barbie*. Have a good day." Have a good day.

Stillness fell over the cabin, as disturbing as the stillness following the earthquake. Neither of us moved or spoke. I brought plans into the void, as though unrolling a navigational chart on the empty table between us, a reminder of an orderly world with boundaries and clear directions. You can sail east, west, north or south, just watch out for shoals, rocks, and wrecks. Head for deep water.

"We should go ashore and start making phone calls," I suggested. We gathered numbers, pens, paper, sunglasses and sun hats and packed them into our bags. I threw in a box of Kleenex as an afterthought. Wordlessly, we lowered ourselves, the dog and our gear into the dinghy. Children swimming from a neighboring boat splashed and shrieked as their smiling mother watched and threw her long hair before her, drying it in the wind.

My husband began to row slow, regular strokes across still water without sound. The sun was in his eyes and his face was wet with tears. My face was closed for repairs.

He trusts tears. I do not, so I stared ahead at the shore and made mental lists. Call George. Call the inn that has the one phone on my parents' island. Hail a hapless messenger to walk across the beach and dunes and moors to tell the Lazears that their son is dead. Find my sister.

In the months of Bobby's illness, I had begun doing *The New York Times* crossword puzzle. I later learned that my parents had done the same. We were all comforted by problems contained within small boxes, the square for the puzzle, the smaller box for each letter, all settled within the confines of a newspaper page. We could rack our brains for the answers to "room in a harem," "Seine scene," "———Lang, Superboy's pal." There was a sense of accomplishment when our frequently sharpened number two pencils filled the blanks, making us think we were accomplishing something, that we were clever and in control.

And so, as Bob and I rowed across Nantucket Harbor, I used my mind to turn the day into a crossword puzzle. Each task became a box to be filled. Don't go outside the lines and don't scribble. Stay in control. Stay in the allotted spaces.

We tied the dinghy to the dock, stowed the oars, pocketed the oarlocks and turned onto the cobblestone street. The first ferry carrying tourists from Falmouth had not arrived. Postcards and saltwater taffy were yet to be placed enticingly in shop entrances. The street was empty but for a dog trotting ahead of us, and a young farmer, early for the street market, sitting on the back of her red pickup truck, and drinking coffee from a blue glazed pottery mug. Her face was framed by blond ringlets curled tight by the early morning damp. Beside her was a cigar box holding dimes, nickels and quarters. Rising up behind her were bunches of basil, oregano, cilantro, tomatoes and corn glistening with dew. She was Persephone come to earth.

I stood and stared, longing to be part of her world, to avoid the phone. I wanted to ask, "How do you grow such beautiful vegetables?" and then buy a basketful for dinner. I wanted to follow the dog up Main Street and then keep walking to Wauwinet, to Siasconset, to the end of the island and beyond. I wanted to be on Prospero's island, not this one. I wanted a world of magic, where things reappear just when you thought you'd lost them forever.

But my husband took my hand and led me down a quiet alley to a bank of public phones. George's message, delivered by Rebecca, included the times he expected to be in the hotel room on the island of St. John where he and Bobby had gone to attend George's sister's wedding. As he answered I felt as though the air had been knocked out of me and remembered a playground event when I was in third grade and fell off a swing. I had fallen on my stomach and been unable to breathe. I had thought I was going to die and envied the other children playing carelessly around me.

As I heard George's voice I gasped for air and the heat of the morning filled my lungs. I wanted my voice to convey: This is the oldest sister calling. This is the big sister in control. I thanked George for being brave and standing by Bobby until the end. I asked what I could do. He needed money to transport the body to St. Thomas for autopsy, then to Puerto Rico for cremation. I took notes as though I were attending a lecture. "I'll wire it right away," I said, as coolly as though he were requesting money to fix a car that had broken down in the desert far from home.

Then he told me the details. "Bobby had been determined to get down here. I knew how sick he was and his doctor had told me that it was just a matter of days. But we decided not to tell him." "Why?" I asked. "Because the one thing Bobby had going for him was his optimism and we didn't want to rob him of that. So all I said was, 'You know, you don't have to make this trip.' And he said, 'I'm goin' to your sister's weddin'.' And you know him, once he makes up his mind to do something, he does it." I noted the present tense.

George's roots are within the Mississippi silt of New Orleans and his accent still retains the aristocratic drawl of planter ancestors.

He began to cry. "He looked so handsome at the wedding. I was so proud of him. He wasn't strong enough to hold his head up a lot of the time, but he insisted that we get to the reception early and he told me, 'You roll my wheelchair over to the table before people get here,' and I did and he held his head up for the entire dinner.

"You know my family loved him very much."

I had heard that George's four-year-old niece, Angelle, went to every performance of Bobby's at a local children's theater where he played Eeyore in A. A. Milne's *Winnie the Pooh*. George's sister Regina and his eighty-year-old aunt Hyacinth, similarly enthralled, had welcomed Bobby into their fold, had revelled in his humor and zest for life.

It had been a long time since I had done the same. From the moment he was born, when I was twelve years old and my sister eight, until his adolescence he and I were passionately attached. He was my trophy. My baby brother. Smart and beautiful with corn silk hair and wide, blue eyes.

And yet, even then his energy level and lack of restraint both pleased and mystified me. There was a perplexing blend of exuberance and desperation in his insistence on attention. His crooked smile suggested that at any moment his act could shift from comedy to tragedy.

His sisters had been trained in New England restraint and rather than join in his robust celebration of being alive we became his audience. We didn't know then that this was the first step of distance we would take from him. He demanded attention, we hoped for it. He talked, he danced, he sang and joked, we watched and listened. Our no-elbows-on-the-table, no-talking-with-your-mouth-full, no-rude-conversations dinner table became his arena. I was both delighted by and critical of his cutting up. I was admiring of and frightened by his flying in the face of the unspoken rules of my home and community that one be self-effacing and understated. He was Henry James's European visiting Massachusetts. We were Massachusetts. He was Woody Allen come to dine. We were Annie Hall's family.

A family is its own solar system moving through shadow and light. Like stars and planets its members recede, return, dazzle, explode and fade into the penumbra. The happy family and the unhappy family are within the same system, moving in and out of crisis and contentment.

Families are redemptive forces when they accept their members for who they are. Or even temporarily despise them for it, as there is always the powerful promise of love's forgiveness, always the profound example of the prodigal son. If necessary the family structure will stretch, bend and adjust its spin to open to those in different phases of the soul.

As he matured, Bobby went from dazzling light into shadow. In adolescence he became a "Jesus Freak," joined FOCUS, a Christian awareness group, and aspired to speak in tongues, a language his family would not understand. He was beginning to give form to his sense of strangeness in our midst.

He was not turning out to be the high school football hero

his father had been, nor as fetchingly popular as his mother. He had neither of his sisters' ease in friendship. He longed for hugs and caresses. Were boys really supposed to be like that? How was he to fit? How were we to connect? For awhile Jesus seemed to be the answer. Where his family disappointed him in love, a heavenly ideal would ease the ache of loneliness.

We laughed at him. My sister and I pretended to speak in tongues. We'd roll our eyes in their sockets, our tongues in our mouths and make what can only be described as tonguey sounds and ask, "Is this what it's like, Bobby? Is this what it's like?" We made fun of the poster of Jesus over his bed. He joined our laughter.

Yet, there was something raw about his pain that made us avert our eyes. A family of such reserve could be unnerved by the chaos of his emotion. Sorrow was dirty. Suffering was embarrassing in the way that death is embarrassing to children. There is fear of contagion.

As a parent, I now understand that we are slow to notice transformations in our young. I don't know if Bobby had a true religious experience on his FOCUS retreat, but if he had returned transformed, we would not have noticed. We would have seen Bobby as we were accustomed to seeing, not with eyes watchful for the new. He returned with a great eagerness to share all that had transpired there, but I didn't differentiate that from his general eagerness for attention. "A prophet is not rejected except in his own town and in his own family and in his own house."

Our failure to understand what he was becoming was experienced as rejection and he would soon respond by rejecting us in turn.

By the end of his senior year in high school he informed our parents that he had fallen in love with a twenty-one-year-old medical student. When I first heard the news, I was delighted. At last Bobby had re-entered my orbit (I was married to a physician); I moved over to make room for him. Then I was informed that the medical student was a man. Back into the shadows.

I made no attempt to follow. I was young and I didn't completely believe Bobby's announcement that he was gay. I thought of his brilliant performances in school productions, his love of drama and role playing. Perhaps this was just another role he was trying on for size and attention.

On the other hand I was not surprised by the news. It didn't seem an unlikely outcome for a boy so hungry for love and confused about gender. I remembered how when we were children and staging plays, he always wanted to be the girl and would act the role with the exaggerated femininity of a drag queen. At four and five he liked to dress up in my sister's crinoline slip and dance around the house. Even then this made us uncomfortable. He wasn't like the other little brothers we knew who were outside slamming their bodies against gravity in contact sports with the universe.

Perhaps all this was irrelevant, but at the time I wondered.

As a family we responded to Bobby's announcement with predictable reticence. A reticence so deep that I don't know if we knew the nature of our feelings. I recall my father's brief flurry of anger as he told me about Bobby's suggestion that he speak with his lover's parents who had invited both young men to live with them. "I'd like to know what they think of their son seducing a young boy," he said. He made it clear that he would never speak to these people, and then fell back into silence.

For all the conversations within the family, on this subject there would remain silence. I never knew how my parents felt about it as I never asked, and as years passed many of my friends did not know I had a brother. There were times when we seemed to live in a quiet darkness where Bobby was concerned. Until his impending death broke our hearts and let the light in.

Whatever the truth or motivating factors behind Bobby's declaration of homosexuality it gave him a striking identity. Now, as well as being louder, more outspoken, more energetic, more joyful and more tormented than the rest of us, he was our polar opposite.

By the time he announced that he was dropping out of Oberlin College to move to New Orleans where homosexuality was less stigmatized, there was little left for us to talk about.

By then I had my own baby and Bobby was moved aside for new passions. Our few visits and phone conversations were forced. All we seemed to have in common was the blood that ran through our veins and his and mine seemed to run at a completely different speed and temperature.

His determination to become more and more who he was, was matched by my own, as though by example we might change one another. My spine was never straighter than when Bobby, in his twenties, came to visit.

We would sit side by side on my chintz couch. He would burn a hole in one of the cushions as he gestured dramatically with his cigarette. My housekeeper would mend it with stitching as fine as a spider's web. Bobby would return for the next visit and burn the other cushion. Seething with rage at what was careless at best, hostile at worst, I would smile and assure him that it was quite all right. He knew it wasn't. He knew the family code. A certain chill behind the words could banish you.

We would sit side by side and I would speak of family. He would try to shock me with tales of the gay life. He did, but like a soldier who won't retreat, I persisted in moving forward, armed with pleasantries as he spoke of friends with venereal warts, raging hepatitis, thrush. He told me how they became infected. He spoke of his sex life and I feigned attention without pointing out to him that I did not speak of my own. That it was a disquieting subject for a listener. Neither of us was real with the other.

When he would join me in family chatter, he would often "repeat" something critical that he claimed another family member had said about me. It was reminiscent of what fifth-grade girls do to one another. An odd sense that to divide is to conquer. That if you can turn the light of love away from one object, it will automatically shine on you.

He would breeze in with his latest beau, usually just the kind of person that his mother would prefer not to invite home to dinner, drop his "luggage," a blue denim laundry bag, on the foyer floor and say, "We're going down to the Village to check out the gay scene."

Was he trying to educate or shock or loosen me up? Back

then, ten to fifteen years years ago, I was simply uncomfortable. I played the gracious hostess. But I was the hostess
who realizes she's made a mistake on her guest list. In that
situation it is the upbringing, not the heart that kicks into gear.
I went on automatic pilot. Automatic smile and, "Will you have
more wine?" When he left, I'd have a stomachache for twenty-
four hours.

On the other hand, there were times when he would become exactly the person he thought I wanted him to be. He
would speak of finally settling down to a career choice. Of
being monogamous. Of doing good works in the community.
He spoke of returning to college. Of seeking psychiatric
counselling. Even as I nodded, we both knew that he lied.
Bobby liked to lie. He thought facts made a richer brew if
generous heapings of fantasy were added. By the time he
stirred it up, it was enticing, but dangerous to drink.

In earlier years, when as a young teenager he would come
from our parents' home in Connecticut to visit Bob and me in
New York, he would regale us with tales of his fantasies
brought to life. "So, I told the guy sitting next to me on the
train that I was a French sailor from Marseilles, and I spoke
with a French accent the entire trip." The triumph of each
such story was, "And he believed me!" He thrilled to the game
of pitting his own cleverness against another's naïveté.

As he grew older I began to find his stories off-putting.
More and more I felt that when I reached out to grab hold of
Bobby, all I got was a handful of flimsy costume. There came
a point when I didn't even want to answer his phone calls for
fear of the false accent I would respond to as though it were
completely normal. No one in my family had ever said to
another living person, "Cut the crap."

By his late twenties he was calling and visiting less. There
were months when he would drop out of sight. If my husband
and I became concerned and called, a recorded message
would say, "This phone has been disconnected." Letters
would be returned, "Addressee Unknown."

For the last ten years of his life, even when we were in
contact, Bobby was our "Addressee Unknown."

As I began to read the first reports of the AIDS virus, I warned him even as I knew that he would pay no heed. He had embraced recklessness as a lifestyle. I engaged in the old, do-as-I-tell-you-so-that-I-may-love-you routine. When it was clear that his profligacy did not abate I turned from him, as if to say, "Okay, if you're going to kill yourself, I'll abandon you first." As though anger could replace love and insulate me against the pain of the fate toward which he seemed stubbornly propelled.

Now I experience the worst of all pains: the knowledge that it is too late to remedy failed love.

I knew that it was just a matter of time before his lie to me, "Oh yes, I'm very careful," would be horribly mocked. Three months before he was hospitalized he had told my parents that he was celibate. Our flimsy trust in these reassurances was revealed in our common response to George's call in May telling us that Bobby was in the hospital suffering from dementia. We all sensed that this was the call we had been waiting for.

Two months later, as I stood on hot asphalt in a Nantucket parking lot, drifting from George's voice into deep memory, I sensed less that this call was inevitable than that we were characters in some fiction. That these were lines from a play, a novel. "That last evening," George continued, "Bobby asked me to drive him over to his favorite beach. We sat in the car, he looked out at the water and said, 'Now I've done everything I came here to do. Let's go back to the hotel.' We had room service, a cocktail and something to eat. He told me he was tired so I lifted him onto the bed and he seemed to sleep while I finished eating. But, all of a sudden he sat bolt upright and screamed, 'My lungs are on fire!' I raced over and took him in my arms, and then he died."

I couldn't breathe. I wondered why they'd turned off the air. Would someone please open the doors and windows and let some air in here? A seagull flew overhead and dropped a clam near my feet, reminding me that I stood under open sky. There was plenty of air to go around.

"George, thank God you were there for him."

"Well, you know, this may sound strange, but if I had written the perfect scenario of how Bobby should have died, it would not have been as perfect as this. He died in my arms, he wasn't in a hospital, he had had a wonderful day. You know, the funniest thing happened, I don't know if it was a reflex or what, but right after he stopped breathing he gave me the saddest smile."

The sun seemed to be drilling a hole in my head. "George, I'm going to go get your money and call Mom and Dad. I'll talk to you later."

I hung up, pocketed my lists and gathered my determination. "Bob, I've got to try to reach my parents." I wanted him to say, "No, I'll do that. I'll do that, while you just lie down and go to sleep. Let sleep take away the pain and reality. Sleep for a few weeks until it's safe to come out." But he didn't. Sooner or later I would have to hear my parents' voices, the sound of their sorrow.

I called the inn high on a bluff overlooking Vineyard Sound. My young cousin was working there for the summer and happened to answer. "Anne, it's Barbie." She was happy to hear my voice, not knowing of the fate I was to place in her hands. "Anne, Bobby died last night, and I'm sorry to have to have you be the one to tell Dotsy and Bob, but will you do that please? And tell them we will sail over as soon as possible." She was eighteen, tender and close to Bobby. She began to sob and apologize at the same time. "I'm sorry, I'll do it right away." I gave her George's phone number and told her to tell the Lazears we would communicate through him until they were at a phone.

Bob and I returned to Main Street, turned up Union past the small formal gardens behind Federalist houses and up an alley festooned with hollyhock. We followed our usual morning path to the bakery where for the past three days we'd picked up the day's supply of sweet, egg-rich Portuguese bread, hermit cookies studded with raisins and citron, cornbread, gingersnaps and small mincemeat tarts for our picnics. By making our usual morning rounds, we could reassure ourselves that some things remained unchanged, that the earth had not fallen off its axis. A mouthful of warm scone would ground us.

I greeted the now familiar, red-faced owner. Flour dusted her hair and collected in the toe creases of her white, loosely laced shoes.

Just as I was placing my order, just as I got to, "And I think we'll take a peach pie today," my husband began to weep. First his shoulders, then his entire body shook. There was no ignoring it. As I continued, "and six sugar cookies," the owner looked nervously over my shoulder. Teenage girls, hired summer help, looked at each other, waiting for someone to be wise.

We women tried to pretend it wasn't happening. No matter what the circumstances, in New England we hate to see a grown man cry.

A grown man crying is like an earthquake. It shakes our foundations. We're relieved when it passes and talk to cover it up, as though it never happened.

CHAPTER II
THE CHAOS OF DEATH

THE CHAOS OF DEATH

We are used to seeing ourselves as ordered and part of a pattern, which, like the intricate design on a butterfly wing, identifies us. You can tell a zebra swallowtail, for instance, from a dark crimson underwing by the different display of stripes, eight on the top of each swallowtail's wing and one bold stripe at the base of the underwing's.

The initial shock of loss is that the design is torn and suddenly we don't know who we are.

Until last night, I was the older sister of a sister and a brother. The mundane statement of my identity, the delicate stripes and colors. Now, brotherless, who was I?

When we sailed from Nantucket to my parents' island where the entire family convened as it had for most of the summers of our lives, I was struck by the fact that I felt like a foreigner. Gone was the familial pattern into which I fit, tumbling back into place each time I returned. Everything was topsy-turvy, nothing was in its place, nothing seemed to have a place. Death had created chaos. I was neither sister nor child. My mother's sorrow made me yearn to be her mother, to possess power I lacked. I wanted to gather her in my arms and banish her pain, to return old favors.

For her I wanted to be the merciful god that parents are for their young children. I wanted to turn on a night-light and vanquish monsters, to offer my hands and part the sea of misery, to take my mother into my lap and make of my arms a sanctuary, to rock away the pains of her world until her sobs were stilled. But I was her child. I was too small.

CHAPTER III
MEMORY BEGINS THE HEALING

MEMORY BEGINS THE HEALING

My parents and George sat in the front seat of the cart, my sister and I in the back. The heat pressed down on us from the black leather, fringed hood above our heads. The brown mule, restless beneath the sun and eager to pull us, flattened its ears, shook its head and scraped its right front hoof across the pavement. Seven members of the Olympia Brass Band, wearing black pants and white T-shirts bearing their name above protruding bellies, tuned their instruments and occasionally broke into separate melodies. A lean, silent man younger than the others, sought the shade of a nearby veranda, leaned against a pale blue, cinder block wall, and played strains of "Mood Indigo" on his baritone saxophone.

Harold ("Duke") Dejan, the eighty-year-old leader of the band, walked over to me and smiled. His gold front teeth gave the illusion of growing straight down from his white mustache. They matched the gleam of the tenor sax he used to gesture to the crowd of Bobby's friends as he explained, "I've told the boys that they have to be dignified while we walk to the church. They can cut up all they want when we march back. But going, they have to be dignified." I shook my head in agreement. I was reassured. Of what, I don't know. That somebody was looking after the mundane workings of the world? That manners were being considered? That somebody was in charge, the way a third-grade teacher takes control of a classroom on the verge of mayhem? That somebody around here was being the grown-up? George sized up the group and took a quick count. There were about forty people in the street and ten more waiting inside the cool bar. He wanted to await the arrival of the complete complement of mourners before signaling the start of the procession down the New Orleans streets to the church.

As we sat fanning ourselves, a young man wearing a yarmulke approached my mother's side of the cart. "Mrs. Lazar, if I may, I will be reciting the kaddish." "Oh," said my mother, perplexed, but too polite to correct the pronunciation of our name. "What is the kaddish?" Thinking that she, overcome by her grief, was not thinking clearly, he repeated the question, and when met again by a blank smile, he explained, "You know, the Jewish prayer for the dead." "Well, I suppose that would be fine," said my mother, not wanting to offend if that was what he felt he had to do. He paused and looked at his feet, and then asked, "Mrs. Lazar, you are Jewish aren't you?" "Why, no," said my mother. He gasped, paused, looked around at his friends and said, as much to them as to her, "But Bobby said you were. Bobby said that almost his entire family was destroyed in the Holocaust."

"Oh, so that's why you called us 'Lazar,'" she smiled. "Our name is Lazear, it's French." "Oh, my God, Bobby always called himself 'Bobby Lazar!'" "Bobby Lazar," victim, Jew, a man of a tragic past. As with all lies, it was merely a dramatized variation of the truth. With Bobby you had to sift through layers of metaphor to grab hold of fact.

The procession leader, slightly stooped with age, donned his bowler hat, adjusted the black silk sash across his starched white shirt, peered straight ahead from under his bushy white brows, raised a baton and blew the whistle to signal the start of the march. The mule cart pulled ahead, and behind us rose a chorus of appreciative laughter. Bobby's friends found it entirely and lovingly in character that he should have left them laughing, that he had taken his joke to the grave.

It was the first time that I was able to see anything admirable about Bobby's fabrications, to understand that his friends appreciated the way he played with truth. To them it was just another demonstration of his daring and brilliant wit.

So there was no kaddish, but friends spoke making their voices heard against the emptiness of the cavernous church and their loss. Eddie Cox, who had directed Bobby in his role as Eeyore at the local children's theater, stood before us. He had been close to both Bobby and George, spending as much time as possible with them "just to catch the fallout of their love." Sweat poured down his face and flowed with the tears as he stood inside Bobby's gray, furry Eeyore costume. He spoke of the delight that Bobby brought both audience and cast with his ability to embrace his part, to believe in Eeyore's rejection and mournfulness.

Lee Fetherstone, Bobby's boss and owner of the Corner Pocket Bar, came forward, looked at our family, and as his voice cracked, managed to say, "Thank you for coming." His gratitude made me realize that others had died alone, their passing unacknowledged by families who considered their child's sexual preference a personal rebuke.

Another speaker who worked with Bobby told how the Corner Pocket had become the most popular gay bar in all New Orleans because Bobby was there to entertain. "You'd walk in and be greeted by a loud . . ." he paused, looked out at the crowd, and said with tears in his eyes, "It's so odd, it's as though I can hear him saying it." Then the voices rose as one to fill in the blank, "Hi, Darlin'!" They shouted and grinned. Bobby-style.

George invited everyone back to the Corner Pocket for a party and en route the band picked up a lively Dixieland beat that bystanders couldn't resist. Soon there were at least fifteen strangers dancing in our procession. I turned back to face the crowd and took photographs as though I were a tourist. I photographed the tear-stained faces of the marchers behind me who carried red and yellow balloons and roses. I photographed an old, bow-legged black lady who danced alongside, balancing herself with a walker and using it to beat out the rhythm of "When the Saints Come Marching In." I photographed a boy, about ten years old, who couldn't resist a parade and added back flips as a flourish to his march. When he caught my admiring glance he somersaulted over to me, raised his open palm, grinned and said, "You like it? Then why don't you pay me a dollar?"

As we walked out of the heat and sun into the bar's cool half-light those who had preceded us turned to meet our gaze with eyes reflecting fear. They looked like wild animals caught in headlights on a dark country road. The crowd grew and stories and bourbon began to flow. "Remember the time the guy who had become such a troublemaker in here handed Bobby a twenty dollar bill and asked, 'Can you break a twenty?' and Bobby said, 'Sure,' and ripped it neatly down the middle and handed it back?" Everyone howled with laughter except George. "I didn't like Bobby's bar personality," he whispered to me. "When I first met him six years ago, he was a bartender at the Golden Lantern and I was almost afraid of him. He could be so loud and abrasive. So abusive of people. Then, two years later when he tended bar at the Harry Dog, we began to develop a rapport and became better and better friends. I was in a horrible relationship with a guy named Scott at the time. I would come in, sit at the bar, drink beer and pour all my troubles out to Bobby who would give me advice on how to handle Scott. I began to get to know Bobby's kindness and wisdom." George laughed. "Oh, my God, he was so funny. Sometimes I just went into that bar so that Bobby would make me laugh.

"When we began to live together, he was completely different at home. Bartending was all a performance for him." A performance that was sold out night after night. Eddie Cox, now free of his Eeyore costume, drew up a chair next to us and said, "Sometimes I'd come here at night and stay for Bobby's entire eight-hour shift. He could sense the crowd. He seemed to know what they needed or wanted even before they knew it. Sometimes he'd show up with crayons and coloring books for everybody and he'd have all these very difficult and often troubled people sitting in here happily coloring away."

According to George, his Bobby, as opposed to the public

Bobby, was quiet and thoughtful. He cooked and gardened. He liked to surprise George with gifts. A book, a rose bush. He was an enthusiastic and insightful reader, favoring Faulkner, Welty and Flannery O'Connor. When he called me on holidays, he would describe the feast he had prepared, how he had decorated the house. On the Fourth of July, he'd hang the American flag from the front porch. He sent pictures of it waving out over the flower beds and small-town sidewalk. For New Year's he cooked the traditional New Orleans beans, rice and peas. Hoppin' John for good luck. It sounded, from my great distance, as though he had adopted our mother's gracious ways of homemaking and adherence to traditions. I hadn't known, until George confirmed it, that this was true.

"When he left for work at night, he'd say, 'Well, off to do another show,'" George said. "He just loved to act. But at home he dropped all that." "All that," I knew from my life with him, was frequent hysterical, loud laughter. Jokes with a sadistic edge. Turns of phrase sharpened to such a fine point that you don't know you've been attacked until moments later when you taste the blood. Playing center stage to any gathering. Insisting on it. "My one goal was to get him out of the French Quarter," George sighed.

But the Quarter was the perfect theater for Bobby. In high school his gift as an actor had earned him frequent parts and rave reviews. If he had gone on to do repertory he would have had to add discipline to raw talent. Discipline was something Bobby abhorred, turning from it as some children turn from a dinner plate of liver. The Quarter prized exactly what he had to offer: lack of inhibition, quick wits and a tendency to overact. Even his abrasiveness was seen by some as a great asset. "Bobby was a guardian angel," Eddie said. "The person that was screwing over somebody Bobby liked didn't have a prayer. We used to say, 'Oh, oh, here comes the attitude police,' when we could see that Bobby felt that an injustice was being done. We knew that the perpetrator would be lit into with such quickness and brilliance that he would hardly know what hit him. Bobby was feisty. He felt that there was right and there was wrong and the difference was clear.

He loved and praised you and supported you if he thought
you were right, and if you were wrong, he let you know it.
That's something I've learned from Bobby. To speak up, to
say, 'I don't care if you're white, black or fuchsia, if you're
wrong you're wrong.'" He smiles, "Now that is a Bobbyism."

In the year that the two of them had been together,
George's reassurance of love had eased the desperation that
sometimes fueled Bobby's act. He had refused to allow his
house, an inheritance from his family, to become a gathering
spot for Bobby's rowdy friends. He had exacted from him a
promise of fidelity and asked him to wear a wedding ring. In
turn, George would get out of bed at three in the morning to
drive from suburban Metairie to the French Quarter to pick
Bobby up from work. Bobby couldn't afford a car, "Because
he was always broke," George explained. I asked why, I had
heard that bartenders made a lot of cash down here. George
laughed, "Because he was always buying drinks on the
house. Giving presents to his friends. And," he added, paus-
ing to sense whether to go on, "there were the drugs."

"What drugs?" I asked.

"Oh, pot, coke, whatever. Bobby liked to try it all and to
treat his friends."

Before Bobby came to live in George's tidy gray house with
its brightly painted white porch furnished with wicker rockers
and shaded by cape jasmine, he had had a series of furnished rooms, apartments and affairs with which he soon became dissatisfied. It seemed at times that his rootlessness
both in love and habitat assured that he would become neither attached nor abandoned. His fear of loss was as intense
as his need for love. As a child well into his eleventh year, he
wanted to crawl into a lap, hold a hand, be hugged. He
wanted the physical reassurance of steady love. In our family
men and boys shook hands.

"You know, he had so much potential," George continued
as we sat talking in a corner away from the crowd at the bar.
It was an old lament. Bobby had been a precocious and
bright child, as well as irresistibly cute with his large blue
eyes, wide smile and hair so blond that strangers reached

down to pat him on the head. He grew into a tall, handsome man with a mind like a terrier's, in pursuit of knowledge and facts as though they were prey. "He was the best read person I've ever known," many of his friends told me as they offered condolences. "But," said George, "he just didn't have the patience to stick with anything. Otherwise there's nothing he couldn't have done." He said it as though it were unfair, which is how we all felt at times, unfair that someone with that much energy and brilliance wasn't doing what we imagined we would do if graced with such gifts.

"He never wanted to grow up. He was a Peter Pan, and he made a lot of people very happy that way." It's true, even now as over a hundred friends cry and talk about Bobby, they also smile and laugh with gratitude for the fun and humor he brought them.

Yes, Bobby was Peter Pan, but according to Eddie, he was "really the Pied Piper. Whatever idea Bobby came up with, everybody wanted to follow along and do it too. He was just ingenious. Whatever he did was just so much funnier and more intellectual than what the majority of trash in the Quarter was capable of, that he was irresistible.

"And he prized anyone whose intelligence could match his own. Or, better yet, surpass it. If you were really, really smart and not being a Nellie Queen about it, he'd open his arms and say, 'Come here, my baby, you're one of mine.'"

But, George regretted that Bobby's intelligence was unfocussed. "Even the children's theater, which he loved . . ." George's voice trailed off, "I mean, he could have been a real actor. Or writer . . ."

The talent for acting emerged early as he put on regular impromptu performances for his family. From eight to fourteen, he was able to make us laugh so hard that we would gasp for breath and beg him to stop at the same time that we demanded, "Do it again! Do it again!" Later this bar became his stage and he played every night to a full house.

At funerals, memory is a live presence moving in the void left by the deceased. It becomes another member of the gathering. The earliest condolence letters written after Bobby's death gave the first spark to this life and it was memory that comforted both writer and recipients. One that delighted us with its perfectly rendered picture of Bobby came from Annsie, his friend since they were both two years old when we had spent the summer with her family while our parents were in Africa. She wrote: "I feel as though part of my childhood has been shaken up and it's a terrible feeling. I haven't seen Bobby for quite a few years but have so many memories. The summer when he stayed with us. I can remember him at the dinner table—milk always seemed to get spilled. But he always had a huge smile. That was about all you could see of him. We were all so short that our chins were about an inch above our plates, Bobby's smile started at one ear and went all the way to the other. Wonderful!"

Milk wasn't the only thing spilled in that summer cottage as Bobby perfected his toilet training and his aim. He would proudly excuse himself from the dinner table and march upstairs to the bathroom. We could hear his bare feet scampering over our heads across the floor boards shrunk and separated with time and weather. He would come to a halt at the toilet, directly over Annsie's father's head. And more than once there was an ominous trickle and then a slow, steady flow through the cracks in the floor where Bobby stood, onto the roast beef or chicken, and once onto the back of Annsie's father's neck as he leaned forward to carve and serve seconds. That night he stormed out of the house, leaving the rest of us to stifle our giggles and stare up at the steady stream that just missed the toilet's edge. Oblivious and pleased with himself, Bobby would arrive back at the table, swaggering a bit as he pulled up his waist band before climbing back into his chair.

"Then the summer of garbage collecting." Annsie recalled that when the kids in this summer community were old enough to row their own dinghies across the harbor, they earned pocket money by collecting garbage from visiting yachts. "Seth [another childhood pal] and I were always mad because he'd have beaten us out and gotten to all the 'good' boats. Seth and I seemed to have a knack for picking the boats that just upended the garbage pail into our boat. How about the turnabout that he bought with the earnings? I can still feel the admiration I had that someone could actually earn enough garbage money to buy a sailboat."

She remembered Bobby's summer job as a teenager pumping gas. "The gas dock—can you imagine sitting there all day? Bobby had enough Tom Sawyer in him to make all the rest of us consider doing it.

"Like anyone, Bobby had so many sides to him. He could have us all holding our sides and asking him to stop telling us a story so we could stop laughing. He could drive us up the wall (his accent the summer he returned from England). I admired his social skils, wondered if he was going to make it up all the stairs from your dock on dark nights. Generally, I'm so glad that Bobby was a part of such a happy childhood."

He drove us all up the wall the summer of the English accent. It seemed that the best he could salvage from his seventeenth year spent at a bleak boarding school on the English moors was an upper crust accent and a new way of holding a cigarette. He was an Evelyn Waugh character returning home to our summer island. Should strangers meet him, they would be convinced that he was just here briefly for a house party before returning to England, to his country place, estate staff of fifty, house staff of twelve.

He would sit with crossed legs (I'm sure he wished they were clothed in white flannel), punctuating tales of his year abroad with the cigarette hanging casually from his fingers. It was *Brideshead Revisited* in a summer shack. I tried to ignore the affectation, hoping it would go away. Behind closed doors my sister and I would ask each other, "How long before it wears off?" We didn't want to hurt his feelings, so we went quietly mad.

Bob and I left the island to go sailing for a week and invited Bobby along. Pretense on a boat is like a dentist's drill, but I remained stalwart and hoped that each morning as he came to breakfast his voice would be his own. One afternoon when we were anchored off Martha's Vineyard, Bob said to Bobby, "Let's go walk on the beach." They rowed ashore and two hours later returned without the accent. My brother was back! I hugged him. I rejoiced. And later that evening, when we were tucked in for the night, I whispered to Bob, "How did you do it?" He answered, "I said, 'Cut it out. You're driving us crazy.'"

Their relationship was affectionate, simple and to the point. Bobby was attracted to and put his trust in exactly the quality that had first drawn me to my husband, an honesty without second thoughts. There were no hidden motives, no masking artifice. We could let down our guard because we knew exactly where we stood. There would be no surprise attack.

Life, he told Bobby, is a love story, you must live it as such. When I would lose my patience with my brother, Bob would move in to fill the gaps. Later there were times when he reprimanded Bobby for the loveless quality of some of his homosexual liaisons. "I don't care if you love dogs, cats, boys, girls or boats, as long as you love," he would tell him.

But that was no guarantee that Bobby would not turn his back or fail to leave a forwarding address. He was, as he grew older, resentful that Bob loved him. After all, Bob was mine.

Bobby was like a solar wind, charged particles surging off the sun and creating an aurora borealis as it sweeps into the atmosphere. Those garish lights were flung across the black Connecticut sky the night he was born. I read it as a sign, but didn't know the language.

CHAPTER IV

JANUARY: GRIEVING IS A HERO'S JOURNEY

JANUARY: GRIEVING IS A HERO'S JOURNEY

Aren't conditions prime? The Arctic explorer looks out on a clear day. Cold enough to keep ice firm, but sunny enough to show the way.

Lewis and Clark are pleased. The wind has died down. No more swells or white caps. They can push on and make good headway today.

Ernest Shackleton tears out a page from the Bible, "From whose womb comes the ice?" and sets off over merciless terrain. He goes for help. Conditions aren't going to get better. His men, in their hearts, know they will never see him again. But they've been desperate for months now. So, sure, conditions are fine. They keep their British upper lips explorer-stiff.

And aren't these conditions for saints? Isn't this when the ray of light shines through the barred windows of monastery cells? When the occupants toss and turn in the night, feverish with the exertion of stalking the soul? Isn't it then that the Lord appears? That Mary appears? That Jesus, a voice in the wilderness, truth and the way appear and touch the scorched brow with cool, dry lips?

Conditions are prime in the wake of betrayal. The betrayal of hope and optimism and the resulting lack of faith that takes us to our beds or compels us to strap on the rucksack and go for help, or stay put and freeze to death.

Just when we thought we had all the time in the world, a voice responds, "Maybe yes. Maybe no." When we've banged our heads against the wall or pew until blood pours forth, that's when conditions are prime. When we've wrung our hands until they ache with twisted arthritic protest, that's when conditions are prime.

When the stomach burns and won't take food. When we're like desert travelers, four days without water and we finally reach an oasis and fall to our knees and sate our thirst at the springs and then throw it all up. That's when conditions are prime.

"Not bad for January," somebody offers, and we realize we didn't notice January, nor have we any memory of November. We have not noted a warming of the planet or a lengthening of days as February melts into March. Conditions are fine and I outfit myself for the expedition.

What is to fear? The monsters. The threshold monsters at the edge of the world. Look at medieval maps and charts. Do you not see scaled demons safeguarding the margins? You can sail just so far without sailing into the mouth of the dragon or the belly of the whale.

The spiritual quest is no picnic. My gear is inadequate. I try to get enough sleep but am too restless to begin the journey. Fear keeps me awake until one A.M. when I finally sleep, but eagerness awakens me at four. Can we start now? Can we start now? First fresh coffee, a rich, deep brew, and then pains au chocolate to turn the coming of dawn into a festival. A thanksgiving feast. Who knew if it would ever come?

But wait, this is not a breakfast for survivors. This is for travelers to French cafés, not to the Arctic ice. Shouldn't I be eating fatty pemmican? What is fatty pemmican? Trail Mix and granola and yogurt leave me thin. I cannot put on extra fat. I do my morning push-ups. I fail to put on muscle.

But how fat could Shackleton have been after nineteen months on the ice? I cannot eat. I cannot sleep. Is this any way to set out for lands unknown, for places beyond weather reports and radar? How will I know how I am if the daily data can't come through? Wind chill factor, Dow Jones average, numbers of Americans suffering from alcoholism and hardened arteries, the ongoing progress of the Japanese. The annual number of murders in Manhattan.

I have to leave the data behind and it won't find me in the land beyond communication. No fax, no modem. It's too cold for ink to flow and with weight restrictions I can only take as much as my shoulders will bear. No lap-top computer.

Are you a fool? This is a fool's journey. You are untrained, but how does one train? You are unfit, but what degree of muscle mass is required for this trek and safe return? Is there any certainty that the correct air mattress, once inflated, will be a life raft? Any certainty that Patagonia's heavyweight, mountaineer's long underwear will keep my nipples from growing stiff and aching from the cold?

Why go? Because, like Shackleton, I have no choice. I have tried to sit it out, huddled here in my tent, supplies dwindling, the ice melting, my foundation turning to water.

It is written that a Hopi Indian tribe stood on a stretch of sandy plateau every morning to sing up the sun. To pray up the sun. Some twentieth-century wiseacre suggested that one morning, just once, they should sleep late. Lucky for us they knew he was crazy.

You put off the journey until you have no choice. The children are crying, "Mommy, please don't go!" You remember those were the last earthbound words Christa McAuliffe ever heard. It gives you pause.

Your men, left here behind on the ice, volunteer, "Let me go in your place." They enumerate the reasons why they are more fit to meet the rigors, to face the unknown. You think if one of them were Ulysses then yes, you would send him in your stead. But not ordinary mortals. Your mission cannot be their mission.

You praise your men for their courage. For their loyalty and forbearance. They have not eaten each other. They've been true gentlemen under conditions that could have rendered them desperate barbarians. For those who perished, they provided Christian burials, complete with the hymn, "Our God, Our Help in Ages Past." You praise them for this. You say that thoughts of their heroic spirits will ease the pounding of your heart as you strap on the snowshoes.

They're always a surprise. Heavy when you lift them down off the wall, cumbersome when strapped to feet used to sneakers, but then they carry you over snow as a small skiff would bear you over blue water. There is a reason that fliers of small planes also thrill to the movement of skiffs and snowshoes.

Your guardians call after your retreating back, "Are you sure this is wise?" You do not answer, "No, this is not wise, this is treacherous and foolhardy," although you believe that too is true. Someone runs after you and thrusts into your frozen mitten, a brochure featuring Cancun. "Only $59 a day at an Omni Hotel."

Perhaps if you could just get away to the sun. A little rest. Someone else calls out that the whole grains, fresh fruit and hiking trails at Canyon Ranch would do you a world of good, why don't you try that?

You don't respond, "But if I don't go, who can guarantee that the sun will come up?"

Danger is all around. One wrong move, one moment of bad judgment can be fatal. But you know your feet, even if you don't know your fate. You, Arctic traveler, know when what looks like snow is merely camouflaged ice too thin to hold you. You can spot a precipice before you fall into it. Once the journey's on, you begin to feel your muscles and your wits.

Small wonder that soul work is done in padded cells. On retreat. Within monastic walls. You could be a danger to yourself and others.

When you are grappling with your soul, after you have made the long, dark journey in search of it, you flail about like a person in convulsive seizure. You should have something clenched between your teeth so that you don't break them. You should be restrained. You should wear infants' protective mitts over your hands so that you don't scratch out your eyes. Grief is a landscape without gravity.

My husband does not know I'm here, afloat. Nor does my

daughter. They continue to communicate through normal channels as though we were all here together on the steady plane of everyday life. Grief is outside the scope of language. I can speak only in signs. The furrow of my brow, the tightness of my lips. But when they who love me entreat, "Do you want to talk about it?" I say, "no," and turn away. I could say "ouch," I could say "it hurts." But language seems slight. The only way I connect is at night when I swim across a river of tears to my husband's arms.

Otherwise I humor them. "Yes, of course," I tell my husband when he asks if I might take the car to the garage for servicing. Even as I say it, I know I won't do it. How can I explain to him that I have absented myself. I am deep within the bowels of grief.

"Are you tired or something, Mom? How can you possibly not know what Operation Rescue is? That's like saying that you don't know who Sandra Day O'Connor is. That's like saying . . ." Rebecca has called from college, enthusiastic and intense. I made the mistake of admitting I had no idea what she was talking about. "Yes. I'm very tired." In my life, that expression has usually stood for, "I am not articulate enough." Or, "It would be too hard to explain." Or, "I am in pain and this pain is not for sharing." It's easier than saying, "You don't understand." That always comes as a challenge to the listener who immediately sets out to prove that of course she understands or is capable of it if you would just try to explain.

I certainly want to live up to expectations. We like to have things run on schedule. The development of our children. The phases of our lives. Our trains. Our planes. Our grief. I am not certain that even they who know me best would understand if I admitted that I was grieving still, or anew, nursing raw, fresh wounds from injuries inflicted months ago.

When you grieve, you might as well be alone on a raft at 75 degrees south latitude and 45 degrees south longitude. Those who offer their arms, shoulders and care are mere mirages concocted of wishes and light. However, according to Dougal Robertson's book, *Survive the Savage Sea,* you will survive if you eat fish eyes and suck the water from their spines and give yourself salt water enemas. These are important sources of liquid when you bob about 6,000 miles from springs, brooks, faucets and melting snows.

You will survive if flying fish perch on your boat as though they were birds and you a solitary tree in the wilderness. This does happen. The odds would seem to be against it, but it does happen.

But there is no rescue. You are not going to spot an Albanian tanker on the horizon. You will not be taken on board and administered liquids through an IV tube, and put to rest on a stiff-sheeted infirmary bed. There will be no reporters outside your door waiting for you to get strong enough to talk. Nobody wants to know.

Spiritual expeditions don't keep audiences on the edges of their seats. Spiritual expeditions will not feed the great hunger for the Victorian-style romance: danger, hardship and beautiful you in the jaws of death. Or better yet: you alone in your small boat with an ice floe one hundred feet high and equally thick coming down on you.

No. There will be no rescue. No high fees from the Explorers' Club or National Geographic Society to tell your tale of adventure and return. You will float and eat fish eyes until the currents bring you ashore. Not necessarily to familiar shores or home as you knew it before departure, but then you are no longer the person you were when you set off. Not the same citizen, and since citizens shape the perspective of their land, not the same land.

The classical hero, answering the call to adventure, set out from home, traveled beyond the threshold monsters into the unknown and returned changed by knowledge. The one who grieves does likewise. But did the classical hero mourn his lost innocence? Did he, as I, miss his sweet, old illusions?

Grieving takes heroic strength. When you would most want to be rigid to withstand the blows of sorrow, you must remain flexible so that you do not break. As flexible as a tree in a hurricane, bending and returning. You have to face yourself because yourself demands attention like an aching joint. You are frightened and you are alone.

You fight demons no more docile than Ulysses' Cyclops, and like Ulysses, you pine for home until you realize that what you long for is you as you once were, life as it once was. Will you ever find safe return?

Will you ever be safe from the pain that was once your heart?

CHAPTER V

FEBRUARY:
LEARNING TO FLOAT

FEBRUARY:
LEARNING TO FLOAT

In early winter we skated so well that observers admired our figures. Neatly cut. Precise. Controlled. With the first freeze we dazzled them with our skill even as we knew we were skating on thin ice. Even as we knew that at any moment the surface would crack and yawn. That the monster lurking below would envelop us as icy water soaked our tights, our sweaters, scarves and woolen caps.

It is the monstrosity of death that keeps us on our toes and twirling, that keeps us executing perfect circles and figure eights, as though control could keep the ice from cracking. We forget that the most we can control is our own skates. I fell through the ice this raw, gray mid-February morning. I don't know about the others. I heard no screams.

On the way to the library to write, I passed the church where I often stop for a moment of quiet before taking out a pen to prick my heart. Is this where it hurts? Here? How about here?

Someone unlocked the door for me. These days in Manhattan there is strict security in churches. Otherwise the homeless might be sleeping in the very pews where you want to pray. We are protected, although it is not always clear whom to protect.

I didn't know I was stepping out of protection as I walked in off Lexington Avenue. The coolness of the chapel enveloped me as I sat down, put my book bag next to me and looked around to make certain I was alone. I folded my arms and leaned my head against the back of the pew in front of me and was overwhelmed by sobs that seemed to come from someone else. The voice I heard seemed to be another's. But the remorse was all mine. "I'm so sorry, Bobby. I'm so sorry." Sorry that I did not love you better. Sorry that I did not love steadfastly even as you turned from that love.

I want to say "*the* shoulders" shook. I want to say "*her* back" trembled and "*her* chest" heaved. I am tempted to turn this into fiction.

Could this be me? Could this be the purposeful woman striding along Second and Third and Lexington Avenues just a moment ago? Could this be the person planning lunch as she walked? Checking out salad greens in the outside stalls of Korean markets, buying a fresh baguette at the bakery, making mental guest lists for dinner parties?

I was left breathless by this attack. It was as though I had stood thigh-deep in a calm sea observing the beach where babies splashed in tidal pools and women in skirted bathing suits set picnics on striped towels. As if, while I watched gentle life unfold, a rogue wave had moved in from the sea, looming larger and larger until it curled high above my head before crashing down on me.

Once when I was a child swimming in Rhode Island surf, I was surprised by a wave bigger than the rest and coming too soon after the one I had been riding. It scooped me up and tossed my legs over my head, it dragged my face along the sandy bottom and launched me skyward before plunging me back into the depths.

I knew I was going to drown.

Instead, I was slammed back onto the beach, not far from where my mother and her friends sat, their long, tanned legs stretched before them. I walked across the sand and lay down next to my mother, close enough to feel her warmth, to smell her suntan oil. "I was pushed under by a big wave," I said matter-of-factly. I did not tell her I almost drowned. The possibility of death was too intimate, too awful to share.

That's how I feel as I gulp for air and try to swim out of the grip of grief into the light of day. I think, "I hope this doesn't happen to my mother. I hope this doesn't happen to my father, my sister." But I know, of course it does.

We skated so well in earlier winter, but now in the quiet days of February there are no distractions and grief grows as though blown in on the north wind. By February's half-light my guard is down. Rain follows snow, snow follows rain and thaws tease and release Manhattan's pungent smells. Pedestrians walk slowly with heads held low, looking more like dispirited refugees leaving home than citizens on the way to work.

Even school children on the crosstown bus are silent. Ten-year-old girls balance their notebooks on ankles crossed over knees. They chew on their pencils and ponder pre-algebra. Their hair hangs in their eyes and their shoe laces are untied.

Except for a wild-eyed attempt at rejuvenation on Valentine's Day, February's inhabitants are like sleepwalkers. The hope is that when we wake up, it will be March, even though we know that March is feckless, wet and grey and ripe for Wallace Stevens's "Depression Before Spring," "ki-ki-ri-ki/ Brings no rou-cou . . . no queen comes/ In slipper green." But at least March holds the possibility of slipper green. February is bleak with absence.

And so, into this gray, silent landscape grief moves unabated. Even the sentinels are asleep or reading *People* magazine at their posts. They do not see it come until they are knocked from their watchtowers onto their backs, legs splayed, breathless, their eyes stinging with tears of surprise and defeat.

"Why?" I ask through my sobs, as I sit in the chapel. "Why?" I demand an answer. But if fate should reply, it will not be in language I can understand. Its language is not ours. We ask, "Why?" and we might as well be banging our heads against the walls for all the satisfaction we'll get. "Why?"

"Why not?" is the answer we hear roaring in the wind. "Why not," if there is any answer at all.

The self-help books tell us: Beware of Christmas! Beware of the birthday of the deceased! Beware of the anniversary of the death! Grief doesn't read those books. It blows up a storm on a simple Tuesday in early February. No holiday. No anniversary.

Forbearance is bred in my Huguenot bones. Our blood flows cool, reason is our bulwark, stiff upper lip our moral code. Give a Lazear a situation, any situation and we will make the best of it. I have been trying to make the best of grief and am just beginning to learn to allow it to make the best of me.

When I was first married my husband took me to his life-long summer home and taught me the quirks of wind and sea. When we sailed in the fog, he could find his way home by smell alone. He taught me tricks of current and tide known only to a boy who had sailed young and alone.

When we went to the beach for a swim, he warned, "There's a strong undertow. Should you ever get caught in it, don't fight. Just ride it and eventually you'll be put back on the beach, maybe half a mile away, but there's no danger as long as you don't fight it."

I have often imagined getting caught in that undertow and I know that even as I heard his words in my ears I would fight rather than float. I am just now learning to float for my life.

Shortly after Bobby died, a friend wrote to reassure, "Time takes the sharp edges off the pain." This was a comforting promise. What I didn't know at the time was that the edges would be worn smooth as grief dug deeper within the self.

Now, seven months after his death a new, deeper pain moves in. To confront it is to dare myself to step into a cage of lions, count to ten and see if I can get out in one piece.

Often on city buses you see mothers and nannies strug-gling with their charges recently released from nursery school. They're hungry, they're tired, they're overstimulated. They squirm in their caretakers' laps, thrusting their bellies forward and their heads back. I remember as a young mother having my teeth knocked into my lips by such encounters. I remember the coppery taste of blood. The kids kick to be released, they slide downward to the floor. They are hauled back, lapward. But they're too agile. Too slippery. They land in a heap at adult feet to which they cling while they scream to be freed.

So was I in the early days of grief. How was one to comfort me? Who was to hold me until I let go with heaving sobs? My husband and daughter tried, but I would snarl and retreat like a wounded dog. My parents couldn't because I was too protective of them to bare either my teeth or my pain.

Today I let go and the sobs that seem to belong to another are accompanied by the true horror of finality, the horror of which centuries of broken hearts have tried to make some sense. He is gone. Really gone.

We fill the world against this nothing. We have babies. We write music, plays, stories. We paint, carve, sculpt. We talk and talk and talk against the emptiness. The human heart gave birth to heaven as it recoiled from mortality and stretched upward to embrace the infinite.

Lear's agony fills my ears, "Thou'lt come no more,/ never, never, never, never, never." His wails a mingling of belief and disbelief. By repeating knowledge too awful to accept he tries to make himself accept the reality of Cordelia's death and yet believes that perhaps just one "never" will be answered by her voice.

Before we can get to a moment in our mourning that is not full of the horror of that "never," we have to accept it. Is repeating it five times enough? Over and over we have to look squarely into that terrible space left behind and understand that it will never be filled. We have to know this and not blink.

Bobby's address and phone number remain in my Rolodex.

Grief comes to live with us as though we'd given birth to it. And, like a baby it changes shape, size and personality, but it's ours. It's here to stay. Eventually it will come around a little less often and make less of a mess. Eventually it will only call on Sunday and holidays.

CHAPTER VI
GETTING A GRIP

GETTING A GRIP

For many of us grieving is our first experience, since child-hood, of being out of control. It is a frightening return to old helplessness and society doesn't tolerate it for long. The collective conscience speaks: "Get a grip on yourself." "Get on with it." But how do we "get a grip" on a self in metamorphosis? We are shedding more than tears, we are shedding skins. How can we "get on with it" when "it" has changed?

Large, red-clawed hermit crabs inhabit the mountain side of a Caribbean island we visit each winter. When they've outgrown their shells they tumble from mountain to beach and trade cramped quarters for larger, vacant ones that have washed ashore. Although I've met them on their downhill journey, I've been spared the sight of their red and purple, primordial bodies, shelless and vulnerable, searching for a better fit. Fortunately they do this at night when we're all asleep.

The world would prefer not to watch while we change shells. We are reminiscent of nightmares, something vaguely remembered and feared. We are primitive and ugly, bright red with our tears.

The collective conscience speaks but those who grieve know that it takes a long time to comply. "It's been thirty years since my sister died of cancer at the age of forty, and it still hurts," a friend tells me.

Another says, "I wish I could tell you the pain goes away, it doesn't. My best friend Lucy died seven years ago and I still cry bitter tears."

And another, "My father died two years ago and there are days when I feel as terrible as I did then. I don't believe in the seasons of grief. Grief has no schedule. It's not neat and tidy and on time."

Our attempts to order it are like Balanchine's ballets, pretty steps, sometimes inspired, giving visible form to the music of the spheres. But they only halt the whirling chaos from eight to ten any given evening at Lincoln Center.

"My mother died when I was sixteen," an acquaintance tells me. "That was thirty years ago. I once asked my psychiatrist, 'will I ever stop missing her?' And he asked, 'Will you ever stop loving her?'"

Can we control this pain? What if we fight its power with our own? Why be vulnerable and naked in our grief? Because the old shell no longer accommodates and will strangle us.

I have wondered lately if postpartum depression is less hormonal than a sharp, glaring, unforgiving look at the truth. Once we have been stretched and opened enough to accommodate and then let go of life, our joy is troubled by underlying pangs of grief. Letting go, pushing forth sets new life on its inevitable course to death. But, we have neither choice nor remedy. If we hold on, mother and child will die, so we let go and eventually, mother and child will die. Grief gets us coming and going.

CHAPTER VII
APRIL:
PILGRIMAGE

APRIL:
PILGRIMAGE

Grieving is physical as well as spiritual. It is an inner journey, but its restlessness demands movement. Pilgrimage combines the two. Nine months after Bobby's death, as I plan a trip to New Orleans, I know that this is no ordinary excursion. This is pilgrimage.

Claude Jenkins, in his book *Travel and Traveller of the Middle Ages,* writes of the medieval religious wanderer, "The pilgrim betakes himself to the sanctuary which is the aim of his special devotion; then, his pious journey over, he returns to his own land and resumes his usual life."

Not bad. Resumption of usual life is reason enough to be a pilgrim. It is exactly what I have in mind as I make plans to hang out in the French Quarter with Bobby's friends, to sit in the bar where he worked, to go see the snow leopard, his favorite animal in the zoo.

Like a pilgrim I am compelled to make the journey, and am convinced that there will be no resumption of usual life until I press so firmly against my brother's memory that his imprint is left on me.

I want to talk to his friends. I want to know of his days, his last and his happier. I want to understand better than I do what he was like.

I ponder the difference between pilgrim and conquistador. How will I know whether I've come to pay homage rather than take away what is not mine to carry? What was private about

Bobby's life is not mine. He made that clear, and should I, in his death, enter where uninvited during his life I am an invader, not a pilgrim.

Eleanor Munro, author of *On Glory Roads, a Pilgrim's Book about Pilgrimage,* also made her first pilgrimage in response to death, taking her sons to the Hebrides to show them their ancestral land—theirs through their grandfather who had recently died. I, who am an enthusiastic traveler am now beset by fear, so am reassured to read that departures frighten her—she dreams of sinking ships and cars out of control. She writes this as she leaves New York City for India. I merely plan a trip south. Where I'm going people speak my language. We understand each other's nuances, our money is the same, and yet anxiety mounts. Each time I've considered the trip I've ended up cancelling the reservations as I imagine myself sobbing alone in a hotel room. I cancelled December and January. I was tempted by February and Mardi Gras, but was overcome by dread. By April I am determined. Yet, I find myself filling in the days on the calendar planned for departure. Obligations that delay leave-taking rather than fear.

I begin to realize that it is not the unknown lurking on foreign, primitive paths that frightens, it is the unknown within. I am afraid not of imagined monsters, but of reality. Mine and my brother's. I dread the onslaught of grief at the same time that I know I must meet it face to face if I am to leave it behind. I dread learning things about Bobby that would make me dislike him. There had been hints at his profligacy. In his carelessness of his own life, how careless had he been of others? What if my heart fails to respond to what he was? Will I then, unable to love him, lose him forever, in a fashion more final than death?

And yet I also plan to go to New Orleans to gather memories as we gather beach plums in early September, a last gasp effort at preserving summer. It works. There have been mornings in March when I've spread the resulting jam on my toast and seen in its deep purple reflections Vineyard Sound shimmering in August light.

I would gather memories of Bobby from his friends, tales

of his high-kicking antics, his humor, his fun. Assurances that he was happy would be a balm to my sense of having failed him, of having rejected him through lack of understanding, a sense exaggerated now that there is no undoing it.

I hoped that as New Orleans gave me a glimpse of his life, I would be reassured that his removal to that place distant from us was a move for independence rather than a rejection. Will I be able to accept that his life was good if he was willing to die without changing a thing? Will it break my heart to learn that like Keats he was "half in love with easeful death" and courting it all along?

George and I begin to plan for my trip. I realize that once he's involved there's no backing out. He's going to take off Thursday and Friday in order to show me "the real New Orleans." "We'll eat in restaurants where they haven't tamed the food for the tourists. And we'll go to hear real jazz, at four in the morning when the old jazz men finish playing in the hotels and play for each other. The walls come tumbling down." My projected journey is beginning to sound less like pilgrimage than wake. My anxiety begins to ease.

When I finally forced myself to go to the airline ticket agency, I wandered from Pan Am to Delta to American comparing prices and schedules. Was I hoping they'd tell me I couldn't go? That there was an embargo on blond women traveling alone to New Orleans in April, or that a ticket cost $1,000, one way? The least difficulty was excuse enough to leave ticketless. "Fly from Newark? I hate Newark!" I closed my purse and headed for the door, I paused, reconsidered, returned and said, "Okay, I'll fly from Newark." The price was right.

I left to meet friends for lunch and as I made my way up Madison Avenue, from 59th to 63rd Street, I harbored a vague hope that I would be mugged and my ticket stolen. In the restaurant ladies lunched as though nothing had happened since 1952. Eavesdropping as I awaited my friends, I heard of problem children, love affairs and difficult husbands. Manicured fingernails matched red lips carefully outlined in pencil. Chanel bags were casually placed on the tables. "You know," said one Armani suited, hair-banded blond as she patted her little red quilted bag, "you can always tell the difference between the real and imitation Chanel bags, can't you? There's just nothing like the real thing." "Absolutely," her friends nodded in agreement. I envied them their certainty. Their perfectly outlined, unquivering lips.

My friends arrived, we ordered pasta primavera, we were served and I could not eat.

Eleanor Munro doesn't say whether she practically starved because her stomach wouldn't go along with her mind's brave determination. The pilgrim's head may be in the clouds, but her intestines are in knots.

To me, going to New Orleans is like walking into Grendel's cave, the darkness I have to traverse if I'm to come to the light. But I'm no Beowulf. Neither are others who grieve, yet we make the hero's journey without a hero's armor, without a hero's welcome and without a hero's choice. We did not choose this departure into mystery.

Packing looms as a challenge I cannot possibly meet. It's as though my security depends on the number of shoes in my suitcase. "Don't take her hostage," say the terrorists, "she's got too many shoes." If I overpack, I won't be caught unprepared, unprotected. I will be ready for any eventuality. Here is a suitcase I cannot lift, but it contains everything necessary for fighting dragons.

Even as George calls to tell me, "The sun is shining and roses are in bloom," I fear a possible chill. Pack a black cashmere sweater, it goes with everything. Pack a white sleeveless blouse in case it's hot. Jeans. Something more formal in case . . . in case what? A funeral? My own? Who knows?

When I arrive at my hotel, Le Richelieu, I find it as heartening as the stands that offer boiling buffalo milk to Hindu pilgrims who walk the horseshoe road of Benares. A restored Greek Revival home, it rises above Chartres Street at the quiet end of the French Quarter. White-haired ladies in walking shoes sit on plush Victorian chairs in the lobby and await a local garden club guide. My room is light and airy and contains a writing desk and antique armoire. French doors open onto a balcony. The courtyard below is filled with geraniums, and a mockingbird sings in the magnolia tree.

I close the draperies, ask the desk to hold calls, undress, climb beneath cool, ironed sheets and soon sleep.

When I awaken, I head out for lunch. Iced tea and gumbo were what I wanted and would find at Miss Ruby's, a small room in an old warehouse where Bobby used to go for chocolate cake. When he was sick, George would come here to get it for him. The night of Bobby's funeral, George brought Becky and me here for dinner and told us what to order. The three of us slipped from sorrow into the strange sense of celebration that is its partner. We ate Bobby's favorites. Beans and rice. Crayfish. George talked and talked and talked. We waited for revelation. He told us that he had been heterosexual. That he dated all through school and that he only began going to the gay bars a few months before he met Bobby. "I could never have been gay while my father was around. I couldn't possibly hurt him that way."

He had known Bobby for four years before they moved in with each other. "We were best friends long before we became lovers, and in fact, we remained best friends. Being lovers was secondary. It was at Jazz Fest in April of '87. We were drinking beer, cutting up, having a great time listening to music and walking around watching the people. We were laughing so hard we could hardly stand up. Finally we had to hold on to each other to keep from falling down, and somehow, we just looked at each other and realized we had fallen in love and decided to become a couple. I didn't go home that night. The next morning Bobby moved into my house." George laughed as he remembered, "I was moving Scott out the back door and Bobby in the front.

"Of course he had a reputation. Everybody wanted to be Bobby's boyfriend and he was known for being fickle. But nobody could resist him. He was so handsome, so smart and so funny." We listened attentively, picking up pieces of a past we had known nothing about. "Once we committed to each other I told him that I wanted him to tell all his other friends that he wasn't available anymore. They were so surprised.

Nobody took us for a couple, we were so different. Bobby was so outgoing and I'm quiet until I get to know you. He was much more of a social character. He was involved with everything there was to be involved with. I was the straight man, he was the funny man. He never worried about hurting anyone's feelings if he didn't like you. I always worry about hurting people's feelings." George switched to the present tense. "Bobby's an intellectual. I mean, he can be quoting Shakespeare one minute and then sing all the verses of a Bette Midler song the next. I'm not real good at rattling off the quotes." He paused to show us the New Orleans way of cracking the crayfish shells. "I think I can honestly say," he said quietly, looking down at his plate, "that Bobby loved me every bit as much as I loved him. We never fought. We always laughed."

He asked if we'd seen the movie *Roger Rabbit*. I hadn't. "Bobby and I saw it again and again we thought it was so funny. We saw it drunk, we saw it sober. There's a moment in the film when somebody asks Jessica, Roger's wife, what's a beautiful woman like you doing married to a guy like that, and she answers, 'Because he makes me laugh.' Well, that's one of the reasons I was with Bobby."

After a few beers he began to talk about the joys of their sex life. "We were always careful. I had been tested for H.I.V. and was negative. Bobby hadn't been tested because he was afraid to know the results. He had lost a lot of friends and he was so wild that it seemed pretty clear that he would get sick as well. But he was such a wonderful person that I wanted to be with him under any conditions rather than not be with him at all. We never talked about taking precautions, we just did and Bobby never put my health at risk.

"In fact, after his AIDS diagnosis in May of '89, it was Bobby who drew away from me physically, not me from him. I tried to encourage him to resume our sexual relationship. I had continued to test negative and told him that if I was going to get sick it would have happened already. But since there were only two and a half months between his diagnosis and his demise, there really wasn't enough time for us to have much of a physical relationship again." He smiled, "But up until that point, we had had great and wild sex." Becky and I looked down at our laps and changed the subject.

I vow that on this visit I will not change the subject. I return to the same table and welcome the steam from pots of boiling crayfish and jambalaya that fill kitchen and dining areas. Sadness and fear have chilled my joints and bones so that I welcome close quarters, cooking aromas, the chatter of friends and families eating together.

I have never liked to eat out alone. I am ashamed of this, as though it is a betrayal of feminist ideals. But this day I don't mind. I don't feel the need to explain, "It's not that I couldn't get a date . . ." On pilgrimage, life is not a popularity contest.

I change my order from creole cuisine to grammar school lunch. Meatloaf. Mashed potatoes. Frozen corn. Corn bread. Adventure will come later. I want to be soothed. Just some warm buffalo milk, please.

I have made two previous pilgrimages in my life. Central to them was a sense of paying homage to a departed spirit. Also central was a fear of the journey accompanied by a driving passion to embark on it. I have gone alone to the room above the Spanish Steps where Keats lay dying. I listened to the sounds from the fountain in the square below that inspired his epitaph, HERE LIES ONE WHOSE NAME WAS WRIT ON WATER. I imagined his view from the window, I imagined the fevers and fear of death. I went outside the walls of Rome to his grave in the Protestant cemetery and sat there through the afternoon and into early evening when the nightingale began to sing. I have traveled alone to Oxford, Mississippi and walked through Faulkner's rooms and pastures. I have sat on his front steps and imagined him.

I returned home both times without answers but with a growing sense of wonder at the generosity of nature's gifts of inspiration and the cruelty of its betrayal as it snuffs it out.

We would be morbid if we spent much time with our noses pressed against loss. The pilgrimage makes us move on as it reminds us of life's cycle. We leave home and return again. The pilgrimage reminds us of the little we know of eternity.

According to Munro it engages us in "the motion of the sun, moon, planets, or stars . . . to share in their eternality . . ." And, "When the pilgrimage is done, if [the pilgrim] is only an occasional wanderer, he returns to the darkness of secular life, only to begin there to prepare for the return journey toward the light that may take place only after his death."

In between is mystery and restlessness.

There is a part of the self that is silent in our daily lives. And a good thing, too. If it made itself known and us vulnerable, stripped of our defenses, moved to tears, how could we get a job? Be on hostesses' "A" lists? Be hired by law firms to execute legal documents? By NASA to take delicate measurements in space? We couldn't be counted on to get from point A to Z in a given work day. To assemble a car, stoke a fire, package a candy bar.

Perhaps we'd be fit to live like the Ramanandi, perpetual pilgrims who pause in their trek only to sleep.

But if that part of ourselves (our soul, perhaps) is silent and unmoved for too long, we begin to feel like foreigners. Communication is attempted but fails. We nod, we smile, we go through the motions of comprehension in order not to offend. Even though this is the land of ourselves, we don't speak the language, we don't know the customs. When asked to dance the local dance we stumble and fall.

Finally an amorphous, painful yearning forces us to strain our ears, but nothing is heard. It is the rebuke of that silence that propels us. It is when we dare to be moved that we go on pilgrimage.

The journey prepares us, makes it possible for us to bear the pain   the truth for which we yearn but whose flame we fear. The journey gives us time to separate from our daily life, shedding association as we go so that we arrive with fewer earthly concerns. If we're staring up at the Sistine Chapel ceiling and suddenly remember that we forgot to cancel the children's orthodontia appointments we might as well be at home watching television.

For pilgrims of the Middle Ages or Hindu pilgrims of today,

the exacting, physical labor of the journey is a reminder of the distance traveled between the world of the mind and the world of the soul. By the blood of their feet shall you know the distance.

But must we approach Mont St. Michel across tidal basins on our bellies? The steps of Chartres on our knees? Is cessation of pain the only way to know we've arrived? After all, modern day travel is hardship enough. If you're lucky and have been able to hail a cab to the airport, chances are the driver will be stoned or have failed to install shock absorbers. The line at the ticket counter will be long. The computers will be down and no one knows how to write a ticket by hand. The plane will be late, and as you sit on the runway, "we're number twenty-five for takeoff, ladies and gentlemen," the lady next to you will be wearing heavy perfume and your head will begin to pound. Give me the dusty road any day. Give me one thousand stone steps to ascend, on my knees and transformed.

Pilgrimage is a primitive and pulsing enactment of labor and birth. They who have traveled in darkness have seen a great light. Jonah is disgorged from the belly of the whale. Dante emerges from the underworld. Out of the darkness of ignorance into the light of insight. I once was blind but now I see.

Now as I travel to that place where Bobby's life was completely separate from mine, I see a life of debauchery, yes, but also sensitivity and the sustaining love of friends. I realize that I had harbored a conceit that my failure of love was important in bringing Bobby to sorrow and life on the fringe. After all, I had thought, as his much older sister, didn't I have certain responsibilities? After all, didn't he himself refer to me as his "substitute Mom?" Bobby, my failure, shamed and infuriated me. No wonder he laughed and talked louder and louder, proclaiming his separation at the same time he was begging for love. He would be uncontrolled if it was the only way he could prove that he was beyond our control. He would become my polar opposite. He would stubbornly refuse to respond to my equally stubborn love or rejection. He would be motivated by yearnings that had nothing to do with me. That were beyond my comprehension.

Not only was I not responsible, it was none of my business.

Now I see that my anger at him for being beyond my reach prolongs and confuses the pain of grief. Now his death reveals the depths of my love for him and I turn the anger on myself. How could I have been so careless in love? How could I have made it conditional? "Bobby's just going through one of his phases, and at some point he'll be one of us again, and then loveable." Now I see the limitations of love that comes with such conditions attached. Now I know that love unexpressed is experienced as no love at all. That love is a battleground and rather than fight it out with Bobby, I was polite. I acted as though it wasn't worth fighting for.

The pilgrim is reborn "to his usual life," for as he is liberated into the universe so is he returning home. Each step out of the self is a step toward the truth within the self. The distance to the soul is as great as the distance to a star.

Yesterday I saw, in a health food store, a book called *Fasting Can Save Your Life*. Nothing can save our lives and pilgrimage reminds us of this.

The reason we have to make the journey again and again, as religious pilgrims return annually to their shrines, is to drive the direction of the path into our thick skulls. So that we can read Jane Brody's fearful tales of health in *The New York Times* and realize that even if we follow all her precautions against cholesterol and exotic intestinal parasites we will not gain everlasting life. Even if we smear canola oil on our doors, the angel of death will not pass by.

Brody is, of course, one of the the most popular *Times* columnists because she writes on the most popular subject: ourselves. Every tiny bit of our selves. Our sluffed skin cells. Our weakening hair follicles. Our thinning bones. The pilgrim leaves all this behind, breaking the cycle of self-preoccupation. We are, with each step, moving out of ourselves and towards eternity.

Munro uses the term "hinge structure" for that device that

connects mortal to immortal life, or earthly to eternal. "The hinge is an instrument doubled that joins. In a pilgrimage system, the hinge structure may be an actual object or monument, an expanded geographical structure, or an intangible essence or symbol that joins sky and earth . . . If natural objects like mountains, stones, and trees, and man-made ones like temples and cathedrals serve that end, so do intangibles like prayers and mantras that rise from a worshiper's lips to heaven."

As the path, the river, the shrine is the pilgrim's hinge structure, so I travel to New Orleans to claim Bobby as mine.

CHAPTER VIII

NEW ORLEANS:
GEORGE'S STORY

NEW ORLEANS: GEORGE'S STORY

I leave Miss Ruby's and head for The Corner Pocket, a two-story, nineteenth-century brick building on St. Louis Street in New Orleans. First a cotton warehouse, then a bawdy house, it is now a gay bar that in many ways is more like a New England general store, a place for gossip and comraderie. Because it's open twenty-four hours a day, seven days a week, there's no lock on the door. The regulars, Bobby's friends, arrive in the morning to drink coffee, read the paper, share the news before going to work. They reassemble in the evenings for drinks and fellowship. For many of them, this is "home," and Lee Fetherstone, the tall, handsome, twenty-six-year-old owner is in loco parentis. He's also a drag queen. "But only for special occasions," I'm told.

As I enter the bar to meet George, Lee and I greet each other warmly. It's the first time we've been together since Bobby's funeral (to which Lee had worn a leopard-skin pill-box hat.) I had been particularly grateful for his generosity to Bobby. He had kept him on as bartender although he was barely strong enough to stand, and when Bobby became too weak to work at all, Lee continued to pay him a regular salary.

His was one of the "helping hands" Bobby wrote about in the first of his newspaper columns for *The Rooster Press*, an assignment that came about because the editor, a friend, was disturbed by Bobby's lack of communication with his family. "Bobby," he said, "I want you to write home once a week and

I want you to do it for our newspaper." So the column was called, "Bobby Writes Home," and began, "Dear Folks:"

"I am fortunate to have the warm and loving family that I do, though sometimes I lose sight of the fact that I can turn to you with any problem or need. Many of my friends here are not that fortunate. They are estranged from one or other of their parents and sometimes their whole families . . . But I am doubly blessed, for besides your loving support, I have the love of my friends of long-standing and the support of a whole community . . . because of our familial and social ostracization, we have had to turn inward and support each other. The love that we are not always free to share with our families, we lavish on each other. When one of us stumbles, one or more of our sisters or brothers is there with a helping hand. We aid our own poor, we comfort and care for our own sick, and, where the rift between parents and child has been too great, we bury our own dead."

Lee admires my outfit and grins, "I don't really know you well enough to say this, but I'd love to borrow that dress sometime." It makes me wish Bobby were here to howl his most heartfelt laugh. I think that he would be pleased that I am at ease and happy here. I think he might not believe it. For good reason. But since Bobby's death I have a new sense of comraderie, of brotherhood with the gay community. Sometimes suffering gives birth to compassion. Sometimes, according to Gregg Cassin, one of the subjects of Peter Adair's documentary film, *Absolutely Positive,* when a heart breaks it breaks open. Bobby's friends are becoming my brothers.

I am comfortable with Lee because Bobby was. I love him because Bobby did. If he wants to borrow my clothes, so be it.

George walks in out of the bright sun, blinks to adjust his eyes to the darkness of the bar and spotting me, takes me in his arms. We hold on to each other as though he is my brother and I am my brother. George has short red hair and a freckled face. He is what my grandmother would have called, "clean cut." So clean cut that my parents were astounded when they first met him on one of their trips to New Orleans. They had not known what to expect when they decided to have Thanksgiving with Bobby in his new home, with his new lover.

I had never gone south to visit Bobby for fear of what I might find there. I had imagined the gay bar scene might be straight out of Hieronymus Bosch's triptych, *The Garden of Earthly Delights*. I kept to the tidy regime of my daily life. I kept my eyes on the clean, certain corners of my rooms.

But my parents ventured forth to join Bobby and George for Thanksgiving, twenty months before his death and eighteen months before they would know he was sick. Bobby was settled, he had a home and the generous spirit of one who loves and is loved in return. When my mother commented on his wedding ring, Bobby laughed and said, "Oh, George makes me wear it."

Our parents found George to be kind and sentimental. They warmed to the affection and respect between the two men. In the past, Bobby's drive for humor, individuality and outrageousness had motivated him to bring a particularly odd array of friends, seemingly plucked from the pages of Flannery O'Connor, "home to mother." A mother less goodhearted than his own might have refused to open the door.

"Bobby just loved the underdog," George laughs now as he recalls some of the strangers he would find at three in the morning sitting at his kitchen table talking with Bobby. "Finally, I simply told him, this was our home and I wasn't sharing it with every lost soul who came down the pike."

Each of us three children had rebelled in some fashion against the proper reserve of our New England pasts, but as in everything else, Bobby did it more dramatically than Becky or I. He did it in such a way that you could not talk above it or divert attention from it with polite banter. There simply was no changing the subject.

So my mother was astonished to meet George, a paralegal wearing gray flannel slacks and a tweed jacket, white shirt and rep tie. No bangles, no beads, no fur or earrings. He was not missing body parts or human language. My mother later laughed as she told me that she tried to act casual in the face of such normalcy, that it was Bobby who burst out laughing, put his arm around her and said, "I know, Ma, I've brought some pretty weird people home to you."

He and our mother shared an affectionate humor that bound them even as Bobby moved farther and farther from her sphere of experience. She had been raised in the mid-west before moving in her early twenties to an all-boys' prep school in Connecticut where our father taught history. There was nothing in her background, from small-town life, to early marriage, to privileged New England homogeneity that would have corresponded to the life her son was leading. And yet her humor let him know that she was connecting with him emotionally, even if she could not comprehend.

This Thanksgiving morning Bobby and his mother prepared turkey and their favorite oyster stuffing. In a New Orleans kitchen with ruffled curtains on the windows and *The Joy of Cooking* opened on the oak, drop-leaf table, they reached out to each other over shared recipes and the sweet, familiar aromas of creamed onions and pumpkin pie.

During their visit with Bobby and George, our parents were seeing, for the first time, their son in the role of Mr. Settled Down. We will never know if this role was for keeps, but it suited him at the time, and it would be essential in the year to come.

Now, more than two years later, George and I sit at the bar to talk, and begin to sense that Bobby might walk in at any moment. I've had this experience before. I've thought that I've seen deceased friends walking down the streets of Manhattan. For years after my father-in-law's death, I saw him on Madison or Fifth, his boutonniere pinned to his lapel, his malacca walking stick swinging jauntily at his side, his beret set atop his head just so. It's enough to give you pause when you're caught off guard, before you pull yourself together to know better.

I ask George to tell me about the onset of Bobby's illness, to share information that had been too difficult to receive over the phone. I had not wanted a disembodied voice reciting pain. He tells me in southern fashion, from the beginning with all the details.

"The morning that I had to admit Bobby to the hospital, he

shook me awake at two and wanted to know why someone was cutting the grass." He leans his weight against the bar, stares straight ahead at the rows of bottles and continues.

"'Why in the world are they cutting the grass at this hour?' he asked and sat straight up in bed.

"'What do you mean?' I asked him, and he just kept repeating, 'Why are they cutting the lawn at this hour?' He got more and more agitated.

"I listened for a lawn mower, heard nothing and told him, 'You're having a bad dream,' and went back to sleep.

"Then he was screaming, 'There's a cat on the ceiling!' This time I really woke up. I turned on the light and asked him, 'What do you mean, Bobby?' He just kept screaming and looking wild-eyed. 'Oh, no! Oh, no! It's going to get caught in the fan. Get it down!' He covered his face with his hands and kept yelling, 'Get the cat down!'

"When I looked up at the ceiling all I saw was that old wooden fan moving round and round and I wondered if Bobby had had too much to drink."

Even George who, in the previous months, had watched the lesions grow and spread across Bobby's back did not consider that his lover was suffering from dementia, one of the most dreaded phases of AIDS. The human psyche denies what it abhors.

He pauses in his story and looks at me. "You know, we were so lucky that we had the time we did. The doctors didn't think Bobby would live past the first twenty-four hours after he was admitted to the hospital, and I thought I could not bear to lose him that way. That he would be here, but out of his mind. Here, but no longer Bobby."

Bobby's mind was always his most admired attribute. Since he wasn't female, his striking good looks never diverted attention from his dazzling intelligence. I was to hear over and over from his New Orleans friends, "He was the smartest person any of us ever knew." And the funniest and most inventive and yes, the most devious. But even that was taken in good humor. They weren't counting on him the way I had. They weren't counting on him to take his place in the family order.

"He's by far the smartest person in the family," our proud

parents announced many years ago when they received the results of their young son's first I.Q. test. It was one of those experiences that in remembering you know exactly where you were sitting and what everyone looked like. Like when the lights went out in New York. Like when Pearl Harbor was bombed.

We were at the kitchen table. My sister and I, aged eleven and fifteen, faced our smiling parents. Warm satisfaction was in the atmosphere. My hands and feet went cold with fury, even as I returned their smiles. They admired intelligence above all other attributes in the people they knew. That somebody was considered "smart," was the highest compliment. When they said that someone was "brilliant," I would watch for the signs. I would sit before the object of praise with a certain awe. I would be tongue-tied and awkward with sensed inferiority. When I was young I never minded that Bobby was smart, but I didn't like that he was smarter than I was and that our parents knew it.

Later, as an adult, I hated that he used his intelligence to play brain games with me, knowing exactly how to hurt, how to disrupt my composure, to make emotional contact by tearing the veil between us with his razor wit. By saying things such as "It's really too bad Mom doesn't like it when you come to visit," he could bore into the primitive, infantile part of my being and bring it forth as a surgeon might hold up a diseased organ for probing and inspection.

George orders a beer, wipes the foam off his red mustache and continues the story of Bobby's madness. "He got out of bed and went into the kitchen. He got a knife and started chasing me around the house. I was really scared and didn't know how I was going to get him to the doctor." He actually laughs now as he remembers Bobby's wild, knife-wielding pursuit of him as they both ran around the house in their pajamas. "Finally I managed to get him into the car and drive him to a doctor who asked me if Bobby had ever been tested for AIDS, when I told him 'no,' he said that I should take him to the hospital and that I should go there right away."

"You know," I tell him, "he told my parents and me, just months before he was in the hospital that he was tested regularly and that he was negative. When he was depressed last spring and Dad came to visit him, a couple of months before he was hospitalized, he said he was having a hard time because so many of his friends had died. Do you think that he knew he was sick?"

"He knew and didn't know. He had the lesions when we first got together."

I am astonished. "Well, what did you and he say about them?"

"Nothing. We never mentioned them. We both knew he was sick, but never acknowledged it. But we knew we had to be careful."

"So when you and he fell in love and you asked him to come and live with you, you knew he had AIDS?"

"Yes and no."

I keep shaking my head and he goes on, "So during the entire drive to Charity Hospital, Bobby kept screaming, 'No! No! Anything but Charity Hospital. If you go in there, you never come out.'

"He was right, even though he was crazy," George says. "Most of the people we knew who had been admitted died there. But I just kept telling him that we had to get him to a doctor.

"Once I got him into the emergency room he kept asking why he was in a laundromat. Then he decided that he was being processed for deportation to a Nazi concentration camp. The terrible part was that while he was terrified and really believed these things, he also knew that he was insane."

A black man, about thirty years old with smooth skin and large eyes, comes into the bar and greets George. "This is Bobby's sister," George says, with the same pride in his voice that I have heard in my own when introducing my daughter. Bobby's sister. The newcomer grins and grabs my hand, "Oh, did I love your brother!" he says. "Everybody loved Bobby." Then he pauses. "I'm just so sad that I was away when he was sick and I never got to say good-bye." "Me too," I tell him, and we reach for each other's hands and cry.

In the days to come, the response is similar each time

George introduces me to acquaintances. Bobby's sister! Now that's something special.

George turns back to me and continues his story. "When Bobby regained consciousness, he told me about the horror of dementia. 'I was out of my body watching all this happen. I knew I was crazy and kept struggling to bring sanity back into my head, but no matter how hard I tried, I couldn't do it. I watched myself in the car as we drove to the hospital, and I watched myself in the hospital and I kept thinking, This is terrible, you're crazy. It was so frustrating and I became more and more frantic as I tried to talk sense but couldn't.'"

George told him that while he had been unconscious George and I had been having long phone conversations following the initial call bringing the news. "Shit," he said, "now they know."

Know what? Half the time we were busy not knowing. Falling gratefully for the makeshift lies George made up as he went along. When he could stand the truth, he'd share it. When it was too much to bear, he made up pretty stories and escaped into them. "Bobby's doing just fine. Every day he's getting stronger. There's no need to come down."

I had thought, after learning of Bobby's hospitalization, that I was ready to hear the clinical truth, so called and interviewed his doctor. At first he explained why he had not returned any of my daily calls of the previous two weeks. "Charity Hospital is just what the name implies. We don't have money for long-distance calls." "Then, will you please call me collect?" "Well, we also don't have very much time. Everybody's so sick, and we're understaffed. Your brother's on the H.I.V. ward because he is in the 'at risk' category. He has pneumonia, but we don't know yet whether it's pneumocystis. We're treating it as though it were while we await the test results. He has lesions consistent with Karposi's."

The other day when I came across the notes I had taken during that conversation, I was shocked by my former ignorance. I hadn't known how to spell Karposi's or pneumocystis, the leading killer of AIDS patients.

Ignorance can be the heart's anesthesia. Slowly, very slowly, as I could stand to know, I knew. Which is to say, there could be hours in the day when I knew the truth and others when I did not.

But being anesthetized can also deny the chance to act. Had I understood that Bobby was in the final stages of AIDS, I would have been by his bedside then rather than sitting here now at a bar gathering memories, trying to make up for the lack of final words. Words that I had hoped would fill in the blanks of intervening years. I have a lingering anger at both George and Bobby for denying a truth that would have brought me to see him one last time.

But, we gratefully took turns believing the lies. They were our naps when reality exhausted us. When my parents flew down to visit Bobby after his release from the hospital, my mother put the question to George directly, "Does Bobby have AIDS?" He looked her in the eye and said, "Dotsy, Bobby does *not* have AIDS." She didn't believe his answer, but she knew that he did. For that moment. An hour later he might have answered differently. He came in and out of denial like the rest of us. In the same phone conversation he would say, "Bobby's going to be just fine," and ten minutes later, his voice would break and he would say, "If anything ever happens to him, I don't know what I'll do. This house will be a tomb."

It becomes clear as George and I sit here now, putting together the pieces of Bobby's last days, that he knew more than George had thought. Knew and didn't know. Just as we had known and not known that he had AIDS. In early July, the same week that Bobby made plans for a distant future, he also wrote his will. Before mailing it, he called our parents to warn, "You'll be getting a pretty sad letter from me. You should be together when you read it."

It was simple and to the point, befitting a young man who had few earthly goods. The pain that seemed to explode in my chest as I read the copy my father sent me made it clear that a breaking heart is a physical as well as metaphorical act. As I read and wept, I kept looking at my husband beseeching him to make the pain go away. He could only do what he would continue to do in the year ahead, hold me in his arms and silently absorb the shock of my sorrow.

Bobby had written in a strong hand:

Dear Folks, I don't relish this and am sure it is not something you wish to dwell on either but—full steam ahead.

Basically, I see two concerns that I must address.

1. Disposal of my personal property. I would like what little I may have to be passed on to George . . . There may be some things of mine that you would like, such as great grandma Allen's silver spoons. We can try to settle these things before I die but if that does not work out I'm sure you and George will have no problems.

2. Disposal of my person. This makes me think of what a strange and varied path I have taken through religion.

First, I want to be cremated. I made a few inquiries and it would be much cheaper to have that done and send the ashes to New England rather than shipping my body. If at all possible I would like my ashes to be put under the chokecherry tree behind the house [the family's summer place] with no marker.

While I view a ceremony centered on a casket, open or closed, as rather barbaric and an unnecessary expense I do understand the need for some sort of communal experience where family and friends may share their grief and give each other support . . . whatever will ease you through my passing is what is right.

Your loving son,
Bobby.

In the end, he was to be as understated as we'd implored him to be in his life. It was all wrong.

I went to the phone and called him. "Bobby, I want a marker. I want to know where you are so that I can go and talk to you. I want to be able to point out your name to my grandchildren and tell them about you." As I said it I imagined a grandson who might look like him, a swirl of blond motion.

I knew that I needed the possibility of the numinous, of sharing the ancients' ability to sense the presence of gods and spirits in sacred groves and prophetic islands.

"Okay. After all, it's for you. I'm not going to be there."

My husband's response when I told him this, was, "He's wrong about that. He'll be there." As Ariel on Prospero's Island. In the sea foam, in the wind and in our dreams.

The concept of spirit is too vague. We need to ground it so that we can concentrate our thoughts in one place. Our limited, earthbound imaginations need something on which to focus when thoughts of heaven falter. The definite location of remains does that. Who knows what happens after death? We have such a fragile grasp on abstraction that we attempt to house and hold it within basilicas, temples, mosques, sacred forests. We force our sorrow into boundaries by placing the names of our dead at the spot that holds the little we know of all that remains. There are those who have never mourned the war in Vietnam until visiting the Memorial Wall in Washington, D.C. When they put their fingers on the engraved name of someone they knew, the flow of pain begins. X marks the spot of our heartbreak. We come to these places to weep and then rejoin the living. Eventually.

Bobby said that one of the reasons he did not want a gravestone was, "We don't know who's going to own that land in the future."

"Yes we do." I made my vow. "It will always be in the family. Your nieces' and nephews' children will spend their summers there just as you did. They'll sail and fish from the end of the dock and play blind-man's bluff after dinner at night. Charades when it rains. They'll learn square knots but never quite master bowlines." I cast a line out into the future and begged Bobby to grab hold.

I now wonder if "the land [is] ours before we [are] the land's" before we've buried our dead there? Now that we have, we are the land's and it is not a commodity to be sold or traded or subdivided. Now that we are the land's, it isn't ours to dispose of. Now it is where we bury our dead. Now it is our sacred place.

"I can't believe we are talking about this," I told him as we discussed details of burial. I said it so that he could pretend if he wanted to. Deny. Change the subject.

Instead his voice was strong. "We have to."

The day before and during the funeral in New Orleans, George rarely surrendered the urn of Bobby's ashes. He carried it in the crook of his arm, to Brennan's for brunch, to the funeral and back to the bar. Through the streets of New Orleans, a beer in his hand, the urn under his arm, George managed the first shock of separation. A container of ashes was his transition object.

Now as we sit at the bar remembering, he says, "I must have seemed like a madman! I can't believe I took those ashes everywhere. And to brunch at Brennan's! You must have thought I was crazy."

"No." I had not. Even then, new to grief, I already knew this was uncharted territory, that old directions would not apply.

Eddie Cox, director of the children's theater, enters the bar, hugs me, pats George on the back and sits down on the stool next to mine. George excuses himself to go to the bathroom and as he walks across the room Eddie nods in his direction, "You know, I never saw a marriage, not homosexual or heterosexual, that was like theirs. Bobby and George were perfectly attuned. They could sense one another's moods and wouldn't tread upon them." He laughs, "Except, of course when George deserved it, then Bobby would give him a hard time and say, 'C'mon, Red, snap out of it.'

"You know, it's just amazing how present Bobby seems. I think it's because he was so present when he was here. I sense him all the time. In fact, people will tell me, 'You've picked up a lot of Bobbyisms, haven't you.' Sounds like a religion—Bobbyism. Yes, I am a Bobbyist," he grins. "Meeting him changed my life. I think I am the only man on earth who has directed Bobby. Imagine anyone directing Bobby! Since he died my career as an actor and set designer has become more interesting and fun. That I know I got from Bobby, being able to be clear about what I will and will not do. I feel his strength and power, his ability to speak out against what he thought was wrong and celebrate what was right. He enabled me to climb out of a lot of problems. He could have been a psychiatrist. He could size up people and say, 'Here's the problem and here's what you do about it,' and he was nearly always right."

George rejoins us and Eddie asks him, "Remember what Bobby used to say about attitude? He'd say, 'Use it like a mirror. If somebody's acting badly, reflect it back at them. If they're smart, they'll see it and straighten up, if they don't, then they're stupid and you should just wipe the shit off your feet and move on.'" They both laugh and as Eddie gets up to leave, he puts his arms around me and says, "Your brother was the dearest person I've ever come across."

A flash of sunlight enters the bar as he opens the door to leave. Then it is dark again and George and I sit in silence, staring into the middle distance. George sighs, "I learned so much from Bobby about living and about dying. He was so brave. He never complained and he made it easy for me by letting me know what he needed to be comfortable and he didn't ask for more than that.

"It took him five weeks to pull out of the dementia, but once he did, he was ready to put his affairs in order. He didn't want to leave anyone with any burdens, and he was willing to do whatever had to be done. If he had to go to the clinic once a week that's what he'd do. He seemed much less frightened than I was. I was so scared of losing him. Then, when he did die, what I lost was my own spirit." He sighs and it sounds like a low moan.

"Our fear, which we didn't talk much about, was that he would die alone. Every time I came home from the office for lunch, I was terrified that he might have died while I was out."

I had become acquainted with Bobby's grace when he was strong enough to talk and we began our regular phone conversations through June and July, reaching across the years to find each other again. He was matter-of-fact, a manner that he had formerly found lacking in color.

AIDS was drama enough. He shared the unembellished facts of his life: chemotherapy, blood tests, the number of pills prescribed and how it was a full-time job to keep them straight. As I listened, my heart filled with love and dread. At last he had my full attention.

In early June we talked of his planned July trip to St. Thomas and St. John. "Go to Magen's Bay," I said, "and just lie back on the water and float and look up at the sky and mountains. It's bound to cure what ails you."

"Magen's Bay? Fine. I'll do it."

The next day when I spoke to my sister, I learned that he had told her that he bought a life jacket for the trip because he was too weak to swim. I cried for the first time since the diagnosis. The image of my brother, a strong, stubborn young man hell bent on independence, bobbing in the sea at the mercy of vinyl and kapok made the horror of the situation real.

Mourning comes in parts. The truth is there and then it is not. There are moments when the fog lifts and the scenery stands before us merciless and hard edged in the sun.

None of us knew that Bobby was confined to a wheelchair. His voice sounded strong. His plans optimistic. But as he was about to leave for St. John, he joked to my parents, "Well, traveling in a wheelchair is great. I won't have to carry my own luggage."

As his deteriorating condition could not be detected over the phone, I agreed with his preference for a September rather than immediate meeting. Now, even as I resent that he denied me this last visit, I begin to understand that perhaps bearing his own pain took all his strength and spirit, leaving none to bear the added burden of my own. Or, perhaps this was his great act of kindness, to spare me the sight of my baby brother dying.

Or, perhaps it was more sinister than that. It is perfectly possible that in the end he could not put his trust in my love.

CHAPTER IX

MAY:
THE GRIEF HEALING
GROUP

MAY:
THE GRIEF HEALING
GROUP

Eight folding chairs form a circle on cold, beige linoleum. A pale-faced pastor and a thin, hunched woman stand near a coffee pot in the upstairs conference room of an Episcopal church. I walk through their silence and extend my hand. The minister introduces the woman and himself and gives us both a few of the papers stacked on the table beside him. "While we wait for the others, why don't you start reading this material that explains what we'll be doing here."

I sit down and lean back against the chair's chilly metal frame and begin to read that the goal of this Grief Healing Group is to attempt specific tasks outlined by Harvard psychiatrist Dr. Eric Lindemann in his seminal paper, "Symptomatology and Management of Acute Grief." For several years Lindemann studied survivors of the Coconut Grove fire and published his findings in the first scientific paper on grief's phases. Among his discoveries, important to us here, is that time alone does not heal. The tasks we will perform are to prevent "grief wounds" from festering. Grief, according to Lindemann, must be fully experienced, for if avoided, it will warp our lives. For the rest of our lives.

The tasks he outlines include:

- *accepting the reality of the loss, that is, getting be-*

yond the sense that the deceased will be home at any moment

  • *experiencing the painful feelings of the loss over and over again until healing occurs, or, as one of our members will later observe, "Just when you think all the feelings have been drained out of you, BANG!"*
  • *beginning to put our lives back in order*
  • *placing the loss in a wider context of meaning, and*
  • *reaching out to others who have suffered losses*

These tasks, it is pointed out, may be accomplished in any order; this is not a twelve-step program. In the very act of meeting here we have begun our work.

As I look up from my reading, I see that the remaining chairs have been filled by quiet mourners whose ages seem to run from the late twenties to seventies. The minister takes his seat and passes around a piece of paper with written instructions. We are to rate the degree to which we have progressed through our grief by putting a number from 1 to 10 in each of the blanks following Lindemann's tasks. "1 indicates that you have done rather little in that area; 10 means you have fairly well completed that task." I'm stumped. I've never been good at multiple choice.

This is May, Bobby died in July, ten months ago, of course I've accepted the reality of the loss. I promptly fill the blank with a 9. (10 seems too immodest.) Then I remember the way I feel when I see a picture of Bobby, or come across his name and address in my Rolodex—as shocked as though I had just heard the news of his death. I recall how each time I talk to my parents, I continue to think of ingenious ways to avoid using the words "died" or "dead" as something Bobby did or is.

It's odd how you can cry and mourn and still fail to accept that the one whose loss you grieve is gone forever. I replace the 9 with a 5. Face it, since he died he hasn't called or written once.

The minister suggests that we open our meeting with a

prayer. "Most merciful God," he begins, and we bow our heads, "whose wisdom is beyond our understanding; deal graciously with us as we grapple together with our grief." I am touched by the tenderness of this plea, so far from the concept of an Old Testament punitive God. We did not suffer this blow because we were getting what we deserved. We are floundering and hurt and we pray for the grace of the healing touch. Amen.

He explains that we will meet once a week for six weeks. That we are free to discuss whatever is on our minds, and are to allow all other members of the group to do the same. We are not to violate each other's privacy. (For this purpose, identities have been altered here.) We are instructed in "compassionate listening," to hear each other non-judgmentally and with open hearts. It occurs to me that this isn't a bad rule for life.

An older woman who is somewhat deaf keeps demanding, "What? What?" Our leader is as soft-spoken as he is pale. His head and shoulders stoop, more from the habit of grief, it would seem, than prayer. He too has seen hard times, you know this from the hurt in his eyes even before he reveals that five years ago his wife died of cancer.

I wonder, did he then, does he now suffer a crisis of faith? A good man tending to God's business as he understands it, defeated by the fury of rampant cells ravaging his wife's body, what does he think now of his God? It is too soon to ask him this, but in a few weeks when I do, he recommends that I read Viktor Frankl's *Man's Search for Meaning* because, "There is the story of a man, who even in a concentration camp is able to find that there is meaning in life. By choosing his response to tragedy, he is able to create meaning."

The minister asks us, "What do you hope and what do you fear as you come to this group?" He suggests that we go around the circle and each speak in turn. I laugh as I answer, "Fear? I fear nothing. After what happened, what's to fear?" Then I add, thinking it a joke, "Well . . . maybe I'll get hit by a bus."

Others are more honest. They admit that now, having been touched by death, they are overcome by anxiety. They might be next.

As a mirage is given life by refracted life, so this circle begins to come alive with stories. Across from me is a tall, blond man, handsome in the fashion of the Yale Class of '50. Nine years a widower, only today has he dared face his grief. "I treated my wife's terminal illness like a football game," he smiles. "It never occurred to me that we could lose."

I am immediately attracted by his authority. His height. His good suit and shoes. The way he folds the handouts and puts them in his inside jacket pocket. Gestures, haberdashery and physique that since childhood have spoken to me of someone in control. Here is someone to watch over me. No matter that we are all here because we need some watching over. No matter that he informs the group that he is here precisely because his control has led to the chaos of his life.

Were I widowed I would join grief groups to find a new husband. It's amazing that more women haven't considered it. Remember the widow in Truman Capote's story "Among the Paths to Eden" who visits graveyards in Queens for just this purpose? Hoping for budding romance, she fearlessly approaches widowers kneeling before their wives' graves and strikes up conversations.

I know single women who join car clubs even though they think transmissions have something to do with tropical disease. They join rock-climbing groups even though they're afraid of heights because, "That's where the men are." This is where the men are.

The young woman sitting next to "Yale" says, "I'm here because ten years ago, when I was a freshman in college, my father died and I never mourned him. He was my soulmate and I miss him so much. Lately I've been thinking that there are things only he would understand. And I'm also beginning to think that my inability to trust men may have something to do with the fact that I never faced this loss. I felt that I had to get on with my own life. Finish college. Get good grades. Have a date for Saturday night. Graduate with honors. Get a job." So much for the accepted wisdom that grief "will take a year." Even if we hadn't been told of Lindemann's discovery that time alone does not heal, we would have learned it today.

A woman in her fifties who was separated from her husband before he died, hangs her head. Tears fall down the front of her sweater and glisten on the pills of wool. "I didn't know that my husband had died until three months after the fact when 'the other woman' finally called to tell me." She is defeated. Her voice is so resigned that we have to lean forward to hear. Even her skin has a pallor that suggests there is no energy to bring it color, as though her very blood circulates against her will. Her once blond hair, fading to gray has been pulled into a bun. Her suit, stockings, purse are all of a color. Defeated beige.

And the others: a bearded, public school soccer coach whose sister was killed two years ago by a hit and run driver. An Ethiopian couple whose eleven-year-old daughter was shot and killed in the schoolyard. "I want to be able to stop thinking of her every minute," says her small, wiry father who does not cry although his wife and the rest of us do as he tells his story. "In Ethiopia children die all the time. We mourn for forty days and then go back to work. But here it is different." Here it was different and they dared hope for their daughter's future. That was their mistake.

Who can stand to witness life stripped down to this core of anguish? This is why we were frightened to come here, why it took the young woman and "Yale" more than nine years to join their grief with others, why my hands and feet were cold with fear before I entered the room. This is what we protect ourselves against with our jobs, our families, our gossip, our friends, our routines. We go to movies and plays and listen to Bach. We fill our eyes and ears with stimuli so that they won't fill with tears.

Tears and rage are ingredients of grief and should the tears go unshed and the rage be buried, you'll think you're "getting on" with life and it may be years before you look down and see that your feet have worn a furrow where they have followed the same circular path. So deep is this trench that when you finally look up, you can no longer see over the edge. One has to suffer in order to be done with it. Suffering only pretends to take "no" for an answer. There are no shortcuts around this pain, the only way out is through.

A young, blond attorney whose boyfriend recently died of a heart attack says of her father's death twenty years previously, "After he was buried, we never spoke of him again. My mother just let us know that this was something too painful to discuss. So now I don't know how to act about my boyfriend's death. What do I do?" It becomes clear that she thinks she has no rights. "It's been two months since he died. I'm back at work full-time. Why don't I feel better? I'm exhausted just returning the calls on my answering machine."

"So don't return them," says another member of the group. "After two months I was still laid up like a sick dog and I just turned off the phone." The attorney looks surprised and asks, "May I do that?" "Yes. You can do anything you want. It's your grief."

Permission to mourn granted.

Immediately after my brother's death, when my mother would walk on the beach, there were a few young acquaintances who, seeing her, would walk the other way.

I have a friend whose parents died when she was ten. She says that none of her friends would play with her after that. "I went to my thirtieth class reunion the other day, and all these women came up to me and said, 'We have felt terrible that we abandoned you back then. We didn't want to have anything to do with you because what had happened to you was the thing we all dreaded most. We were afraid it was catching.'"

No one likes to peer into suffering's eye. It burns a hole in the carefully woven fabric of our civility. It pierces our hearts and leaves us speechless. "I'm sorry" seems so inadequate but it's all we've got. It was that promise of pain and our own inadequacy that made us reluctant to meet in this group today. We were not prepared to see our hearts in others' faces.

According to the leader of our group, we can be this afraid for a long time, "You can become the walking wounded, wooden and hostile." We can walk that way to our graves. Society allows and even approves of it.

The good, strong men of my New England childhood, models of restraint, got on with their lives in spite of hardship and loss. I am shocked now to look back at the hot coals of emotion they walked across without a whimper. A brother's suicide. A stillborn son. Parental deaths noted with one day off and a crisp memorial service from the Book of Common Prayer. A child drowned at camp.

And the women with all the same losses and miscarriages borne with strength and dignity. No wonder that we were surprised when we, the children, became adults and discovered how much loss hurts.

But we knew to march on. The longest march, through pain. I now realize that if we keep marching dry-eyed and determined we'll never come to the end of our journey, that we're like caged gerbils on exercise wheels, fooled by movement into thinking we're going somewhere.

This is the legacy I bring to the Grief Group, so when it is time for me to tell my own story, I do so tearless and smiling. I rise to the occasion, displaying a fine wit, sharp even in adversity. I show off my courage and my humor. I think, "My father would be proud of me," as though I were an eight year old climbing back on the horse. It is the others' stories that make me cry, not my own. It is permissible to grieve for others, that's called compassion. Crying for yourself is a different matter. That's called self-pity.

Earlier today I was surprised and wrinkled my nose in distaste when my husband told me about the funeral rites of a friend's mother, an orthodox Jew. "There was wailing and rending of garments," he said. "Oh, I wouldn't like that," I replied. "I wouldn't want to be that out of control." My husband disagreed. "At least they know what they're supposed to do."

Well, I certainly don't. I make it up as I go along. One of my most striking memories of the early days of Bobby's illness was of smiling as I answered a friend who had asked why I looked so sad. "I just found out my brother has AIDS." I smiled. I shrugged. I lifted my palms up to the pale blue ceiling of our favorite coffeehouse. I smiled as if to say, "But I'm no Job." I smiled as if to say, "Of course this isn't real." I smiled to say, "This is more than I can bear, so we won't bear it, we will move on to talk of other things." I smiled to say, "This can't be happening. Soon the clowns will fire the guns and little flags will pop out." I smiled waiting for the joke.

The expression of sadness, horror and sympathy in her eyes made me feel that I was the clown arriving at the wrong party.

It's a wonder anyone can comfort anyone else in their grief. What was my friend to do when she could see from my bony shoulders, drawn face and limp hair that I was in deep distress, yet sat across from her smiling? Was she to smile in return? She did not, and perhaps the best the outsider can do is to express those feelings the mourner can't.

Here in the Grief Healing Group no one shies away from sobs and misery. Here tears "roll down like mighty waters." When I tell the other members that just the other day someone close to me grew impatient and said, "You can't possibly still be grieving. You and your brother weren't even that close," there is a unaminous nodding of heads. "Nobody wants to be with a sad person," says the attorney. "They grow impatient after two weeks."

My friend was not wrong, my brother and I were not close. The passion of our attachment when he was a young boy turned to later disenchantment. Now that old passion returns and fuels my remorse. I turn the anger, that integral aspect of grief, against myself. Whereas many mourners shake their fists in fury at the space their beloveds have left behind— "How could you go and leave me?"—I am my own accuser. Why had I not been larger-hearted? Why hadn't I included Bobby in my life? Why had there been limits and conditions on my love? I become aware of my most grievous crime: I had been ashamed of him.

Now I am ashamed of myself. Such guilt and ambivalence complicate and extend grief. But how could an outsider understand that no, my brother and I were not close and that is precisely why I grieve.

The meeting ends and "Yale" and I stand together waiting for the elevator. We've headed straight to each other with smiles of recognition. We are brother and sister. The prototypically restrained WASPs. One has an instinct for it, can sniff out the scent of Yankee rectitude. I see it in the park all the time. When the dogs are off their leashes, the poodles run to the poodles, the labradors to the labradors and the amazed owners comment, "I swear they know their own. It happens every time." You don't need graduate degrees in zoology, just eyes in your head to know it.

It becomes clear that the two of us came here under false pretenses. He laughs, "You know, when I decided to join this group, I thought it was because my story would help the other people." I nod and smile, "I came because I thought it would be 'good for my writing.' It was strictly 'research.'"

Neither of us is being coy. I really thought that I had proceeded far enough through my grief to not be in need of a group "healing experience." I believed, however, that the other lives and deaths would broaden my scope. I was not coy, but grief was.

Grief played games with "Yale" for nine years while he raised a family, remarried, divorced, became an alcoholic and then a recovering alcoholic. The way grief figured it was, "If he wants to ignore me, let him. I've got staying power," then made a slow and steady chaos of his life. Even tonight grief had been in hiding until we looked across the circle at the tear-streaked face of the Ethiopian mother and saw ourselves.

I am like photographers who separate themselves from experience in the very act of capturing it, their instruments keeping it at arm's length. When Margaret Bourke-White was asked how she could stand to photograph Buchenwald and Leipzig-Mochau, she replied, "Sometimes I have to work with a veil over my mind. When I photographed the murder camps the veil was so tightly drawn that I hardly knew what I had taken until I saw the prints of my own photographs."

A writer's mind is her camera, capturing chaos into organized studies. A writer is the guy in sequined tights surrounded by twelve tigers in a ring. His only defenses against clawed slaughter are a whip and wits. The tiger-tamer, the ultimate controller of raw, savage life knows that if he blinks he could be dead. I've often wondered if he should do it in front of the children.

In the intervening week between meetings, I miss the other members of the group. It's as though fellow sufferers are coated with Krazy Glue, the bonding is so swift and secure. And yet, when we reassemble and the minister asks, "Have you had any thoughts this week that you would like to share with the rest of us?" he is met by silence. He encourages, as one might a shy child, "About our meeting?" Silence. "About this group?" Some of us stare into the middle distance. Others study their shoes. As a minister he is used to silence. It neither provokes nor challenges him. It hovers in the middle of our circle.

Of course we all had had plenty of thoughts during the week, but if we were people who found it easy to talk, we wouldn't be here in the first place. We would have made our grief known long ago, we would have shouted it from the rooftops until someone raised a window to protest, "Shut up! People are trying to sleep!" If we'd responded, "Sure, I'll shut up when I've finished shouting," we wouldn't be here.

Since I am a good hostess, trained in keeping-the-ball-rolling, I raise my hand.

"Yes, Barbara?"

Hearing my name makes me want to retreat, but I proceed and tell of a searing pain in my leg and spine and a consequent consultation with a neurologist. "Medically there were no findings. Emotionally there were."

Thunk! As the small, cold hammer made contact below my knee my leg shot forward. I was doing something right. "Are you sure I'm not faking this?" I asked my friend and physician.

"You can't," he said and gave my other knee a quick whack. He stuck pins into the soles of my feet. "Can you feel that?"

"Yes."

"Any difference between the sensations in the two feet?"

"No."

"This one?" repeating the test. "Now this one?" A pin jab to the left big toe. Now the right. I knew he would discover that I was a fraud, that I was malingering, that I was . . . I failed to hear his next instruction. "Pardon me?"

"Lift this leg," he repeated and pushed against it as I complied. He was pleased. "Now stand up and bend forward."

The examination was completed and he sat down, sighed, and folded his hands. We were ready to confer. "You are neurologically perfect," said he and began to ask about stress in my life. When I told him of Bobby's illness and death, he nodded, "My sense is that it has taken the terrible pain of that loss this long to settle into your body."

I knew he was right and didn't protest. He continued, "I see athletes all the time who play with broken bones and concussions and they don't know until the game is over how much pain they've been in. I think that's what happened to you." I wanted to ask, "Is the game over?" I wanted some reassurance.

"Can you possibly take a vacation? Get away for awhile?" Since the prescription was pleasant and the prognosis good, why did the news depress? Because here was another startling reminder that the abiding effects of grief were beyond my control. It was a conceit that control had been working at all. I kept thinking of a line from Yeats: "Things fall apart, the center will not hold."

My center has collapsed. I'm too young for a heart attack, which would provide the correct metaphorical fit. No. Instead, the manifest message is that I have no backbone. I am spineless before grief. Or that I don't have the stomach for it. For days my stomach has curled itself into a defensive knot, as though to ward off another kick.

Illness as metaphor acts itself out on the stage of grief and I grow embarrassed as I, the audience, see such obvious rendering.

I am ashamed and realize every part of my intellect and training struggles against the acceptance, the stillness, the defeat demanded by grief. When things fall apart, I rush to fix them. I am responsible. I know my job. If the center is not holding I throw my weight against it without stopping to consider the discrepancy between its weight and my own.

I think of the happily stoned and bearded youths who crowded the steps of Alleys General Store on Martha's Vineyard through the balmy summers of the '60s and '70s. "Hey man, mellow out." "Smile." "Everything's groovy."

I was usually rushing up those steps with a baby clutched to my hip, and back down again with baby and coffee, milk, cream, fresh fruit, *The New York Times,* the things that keep a vacation house moving from picnic to picnic.

Everything seemed groovy to them and I was in need of chilling out, but was too full of youthful determination to grab life, wrestle it to the ground and stand triumphantly with one foot on its back.

I am no longer in my twenties and early thirties and am learning that life will not necessarily comply. My scope has narrowed. If I get dinner prepared, a satisfactory page of writing done, the dog walked, and if my husband and daughter feel loved, I consider that a triumph.

But with grief you cannot count such sweet success. No sooner do you say, I'm doing swell, no sooner have you caught yourself laughing than you hear your exhale as a sob.

You cannot put grief in perspective because it has no perspective. You, unlike Dürer with his model, cannot hold a grid before it, take its measure and order it with pigment and form. You won't find grief ornately framed and softly lit on a wall at the Frick.

Which is not to say there haven't been noble attempts. Michelangelo's *Pieta* succeeds in giving the mystery form, grief and acceptance mingling as though marble were water.

But my life is not sculpted and even the most ordinary things seem to be falling apart. When we went to the refrigerator for milk the other night, it fell into our glasses in sour curds. There is a message on my answering machine, "Mrs. Ascher, this is the dentist's office. You were due here an hour ago."

Where am I when I need me? I await rescue. Why won't it come? Although the neurologist suggested I get away he failed to book the flight. I suggest Bermuda to my husband who's unable to leave town. Will nobody save me? Of course, I know the answer, but knowing and living answers are two different things.

When I was in law school and running a household and caring for a family, I began to falter. I cried and my husband said, "Just keep rowing your boat and you will get to shore."

I know this is true now. But shouldn't there be extra crew on board? I'm the only one in this particular boat. I neglected to hire a relief oarsman, and without a navigator, how will I know if I'm headed for shore or sea?

Won't somebody save me? Of course the answer is I will save myself. Maybe not today. Maybe not even this week or next month. And I don't know how I'll do it, but I've learned a few life-saving techniques to be used when bobbing about, alone at sea. The first aid kit contains back issues of *The New York Times* crossword puzzles and a few thrillers. When Bobby got sick I read *The Silence of the Lambs,* and found comfort in its graphic viciousness. As long as the book lasted I could forget the viciousness about me. As long as the fictitious serial killer was on the loose, I could forget the real serial killer, AIDS, that was stalking my brother. I bought an extra copy and sent it to my parents.

After his death I reread the Book of Job and joined a study group that was discussing it. I read the *Iliad* and *King Lear* before moving on to books about the holocaust. I read Elie Wiesel. Charlotte Delbo. Primo Levi. Aharon Appelfeld. Ida Fink. I found company in their struggles to break through the isolation of experience for which there is no language, of pain that propels but words that fail. Are there words for death in life? Claude Lanzman, director of *Shoah,* a film about the holocaust, writes that there are not. "I have precisely begun with the impossibility of telling this story."

At first, I could not even feel my story. Then I only felt it. In time the words came, imprecise and faltering. The relationship of the language of grief to the language of everyday life is that of dreams to reality. Grief is experienced in metaphor.

Metaphor filled in my blanks. Serial killers. Nazi killers. The triumph of evil over good. Worlds in chaos. I wonder now, what was the holocaust-as-metaphor for Bobby? The holocaust which, according to his tale, had destroyed most of his family. What was his pain beyond words?

As I read I searched not just for language to match experience, but for an answer I knew I wouldn't find. Where was God in all this? There were times when I echoed Glouster's wail of betrayal in Lear, "As flies to wanton boys are we to the gods. They kill us for their sport." One day as I walked in the country, my rage at the senselessness of it all grew with each step until I stood in the middle of a winter-browned pasture, raised my arm above my head and shook my fist at the gray sky. "God," I shouted into the emptiness, "Why don't you come out and fight like a man?"

I want to follow the neurologist's advice and put physical distance between myself and pain, but it's tricky for a woman traveling alone. The choices are nunneries or spas unless you want to be vulnerable to pickups or the extreme loneliness caused by being surrounded by honeymooners. I've had both experiences and do not choose to repeat them.

I've found that it helps to have one foot in antiquity when trouble is breaking out all around. This morning I read about the restored statue of Marcus Aurelius astride his horse, being returned to its original sixteenth-century site on the Capitoline Hill in Rome. Forty thousand people came to view it the first day. I am not alone in my yearning for continuity.

There was a warm May day, two years ago, when my daughter and I lay down in the wild fennel, between columns and ruins on that hill. The sun shone on our closed eyelids as our minds stretched back through centuries. Perhaps if I could do that, I would be able to, as Lindemann suggests, put my grief and my life in a larger context.

Friends suggest Florida. "Palm Beach is just two-and-a-half hours away." But Palm Beach has no fields of fennel, what could it tell me of eternity? Others suggest spas. But I want to get away from me. I want to focus on the larger picture. I want to know how it all fits.

I dream of Venice. Perhaps the chaos of the universe would be stilled if I set my sites on Titian's raucous *Dinner at the*

House of Levi or Bellini's serene madonna in the cool quiet of San Zachariah. Perhaps simply being on the Grand Canal watching the rush of tides to and from the sea, maybe then I would sense harmony where now there is only discord.

I tell all this to the group and then fall silent. The high school coach blinks. "I can't believe you're saying this about the pain in your leg. Last year, as the first anniversary of my sister's death got closer, I began to have chest pains. The doctors couldn't find anything wrong." He paused for breath. "This really concerned me because I've never been sick. I've never been in pain. And lately I've been having all sorts of aches and pains."

The attorney says, "The lump in my throat hurts so much that I've been thinking that I have throat cancer."

Grief is physical and it hurts. Coach and I sigh and settle back in our chairs, like lovers returning to separate pillows after lovemaking. We are not alone in this world.

CHAPTER X
IF ONLY

IF ONLY

The minister opens the third meeting of the group, "Today we're going to talk about guilt, which is a natural aspect of the grieving process."

"A natural aspect of the living process," I mutter.

Coach responds, "I had a pretty guilt-free childhood. If I did something wrong or felt bad about something, it was all out in the open. My parents and I would discuss it and that would be that. But now . . ." he smiles and then begins to cry, lifts his hands helplessly and adds, "But now I'm guilty and anxious almost all the time."

The older woman who is widowed and nearly deaf says that she cannot sleep for the fears of the night. The attorney wonders if she'd agreed to marry her boyfriend, would it have prevented his heart attack? "I know it's silly, but I wonder if he died of a broken heart?"

"Yale" says that liquor numbed his guilt and anxiety. Temporarily.

The Ethiopians ponder, "If we hadn't come to America . . ."

"The trouble with death is all the loose ends," says Coach. The things said and unsaid. We have, in the words of the confession in the Book of Common Prayer, left undone those things we ought to have done, and done those things we ought not to have done.

Too many loose ends. They fly about, like maypole streamers abandoned by young girls fleeing a brewing storm. How to wrap them up? By forgiving ourselves the unfinished business.

I am far guiltier about what I did not do than what I did do with respect to Bobby's life. This continues to be the ongoing discussion my husband and I have late into the nights. His pain is different but frequently echoes my own. "I should have gone to New Orleans," says he. "Even if it wouldn't have made the slightest difference, I should have made more of an effort to see him, to talk to him. I loved him so much and I know he knew that, but that makes it all the more inexcusable." What is "it?" Our neglect? Our inability to change a course of events that Bobby was determined to control? Our inability to control his lack of control? Our failure to love more generously? We list, like a litany, all the efforts we should have made but didn't because we were overworked, tired, busy with our own lives. "Phooey," my husband now says, dismissing all those excuses.

He remembers Bobby as a young boy who when visiting us would crawl into his lap. In those days we made room for him. But somehow the quarters of our hearts became cramped and now we weep for having failed to expand them. Our ears fill with tears as we lie on our backs, making confessions to the night.

Even when death is not entirely unexpected there is unfinished business. Shyness, old grudges, personal style stand in the way. I tell the group about a minister who spoke to friends gathered about the bedside of a talented editor dying of lung cancer. "This is not a time to be reticent. Speak your mind," she had said. "Say whatever you feel, whether it's, 'I'm so sad you're dying, I'll miss you so much,' or, 'I love you, you've been a wonderful friend.'" I now realize that her advice was for the future mental health of the grief-stricken. She gave them permission to dispense with life-long training in denial and stiff upper lips. They were told, not only that they were allowed to speak from their hearts, but that they must.

But when your sister falls under a drunk driver's wheels, when your child is murdered, when your thirty-five-year-old boyfriend suffers a fatal heart attack, when AIDS kills your brother faster than expected, when death gallops through town at breakneck speed, you're left with your mouth open, choking on all that was left unsaid.

Each one of us here is guilty of past silences, and each afflicted with punitive anxieties. In the days before everything settled into the nerve endings of my spine, when anxiety was free floating, I would awaken from an afternoon nap with my heart pounding and would have to lead myself step by step to reality as though it were a distant oasis. "Neither you nor your life are a mirage," I would reassure. "You are at home where you are safe. Your dog is here," albeit asleep on his back with his ears spread like wings, his hind legs splayed and his front paws folded in submission. But yes, even flat on his back, your dog is here and might respond if real rather than imaginary monsters entered.

I would walk to the kitchen and stare out the window over rooftops and down onto the familiar avenue where I've lived for twenty-three years. My eyes would travel across the landmarks and familiar sights. A grocery store, a deli, young girls with knee socks drooping around their ankles as they walked home from the private school up the street. At six, seven and eight years old they looked exactly as my daughter had at the same ages. Same uniform, same untied laces, same book bags weighing down one side of their bodies. The familiarity eventually slowed the beats of my heart.

Last year on February 14, my birthday, Bobby's weekly newspaper column was entitled "To My Special Valentine Sister." I was taken aback by this tug into his life across our distance and differences.

"Dear Barbie:" it began and went on to recall his sadness, when I, at age fourteen and he three, left home for boarding school. "Visits to you . . . as well as your trips home, were so special to me . . . There was a great deal more maternal bonding between us than any sibling rivalry. And while Mom had Dad, I didn't have to 'share' you with anyone. Small wonder I became heartbroken upon discovering that you were going away. Did Mom ever tell you how I cried one night because you were going away? Ah, the futility of the memories of tears!"

Reading this reminded me of another time when he reexperienced this intense sense of abandonment when he was nine and I left to be married.

He and I stayed up late the night before my wedding. As my eyes grew heavy with sleep, his grew wider with urgency. His grip on me became more frantic with the hours. We played Go Fish, we played Hearts, we played Crazy Eights.

He was Scheherazade, holding off the inevitable by keeping me at his side, awake and engaged. But unlike Scheherazade, he wished morning would never come. Much of the rest of his life would be spent this way, entertaining wakefulness to keep loneliness from the door. He would party all night, he would work the late shift at the bar. He would laugh and play until exhaustion left no room for regret and then he would sleep.

I am relieved to remember that night of Crazy Eights because later there were times when I failed to stand watch with him, when I dismissed the needs of a seventeen, nineteen or twenty year old as I could not a nine year old's.

These days the failures are cast in color on a giant screen, the kind they had at drive-ins when we were kids and could see the picture from miles away. I see his expression. I see my own. I see my preoccupation. I see his beseeching eyes. He might as well be saying, "Wanna play a game of Hearts?" Sorry kid, my heart is elsewhere.

Not that it matters, just as the details of nightmares only matter if you're five days a week on the analyst's couch, but I can tell you every burning bright detail of the last such encounter.

It is June, 1988, and I am driving up the driveway to a Connecticut inn where my father is to be honored at a retirement party. There is Bobby standing under the canopy. I only ask now, how long had he been standing there? I only know now that he was waiting for me.

When I still lived at home, he used to stand at the window, the tip of his small nose flattened against the glass, his lips askew, as he waited for me to return from school. I don't know if he continued to do this after I went away to prep school only to return for holidays. What he wrote in his newspaper column makes me fear that he did.

This day in Connecticut I respond to his enthusiastic greeting with a brief hug. Even at thirty he is like a puppy in his eagerness and I pull away from it. I ask, "Where shall I take my suitcase?" "I'll take it for you. Do you want me to park the car?" I let him take my bag while I find a parking space, then enter the lobby and tell him, "I'd better go get dressed. I'll see you later," and make a hasty retreat.

Retreating from what? His need? The pain in his eyes? The fear that he might launch into an act, playing all the parts, shutting me out at the same time he insists on my attention? Whenever he assumed roles I wanted to shout, "Cut! Just be normal!"

Since reticence is the family code, he had learned to read the signs. In our familial language the spoken word was often persiflage to distract from the unspoken truth. Our words were like birds diving, soaring and singing far from the nest to divert attention away from what was vulnerable. So there is no need for me to say, "act normal," he knows that's what I want and he grows quiet and sad.

It seems that at an early age Bobby determined that one of his roles in the family was to be the funhouse mirror that deforms and exaggerates what it reflects. Our mother's femininity could be reflected back as a screaming queen, our father's flirtatiousness with women as a tease of men, my reserve as cold remove. We averted our eyes. That day in Connecticut I averted my eyes for fear I would see my reflection.

I also looked away because I saw what my mind refused to assimilate. Bobby had too many moles on his face. I was certain that they had not been there before. Only now do I wonder whether he had grown the new mustache and beard to cover the Karposi's lesions, as camouflage for the evidence of despair.

Each of us in the grief-healing group has experienced the if-only stage of grief. Over and over I think, if only I had not been so distant. If only I had insisted on intimacy and involvement. If only I had not run from the pain in his eyes during that last visit. If only I had moved toward rather than away from it by putting my arms around him, by telling him that I loved him and had always loved him. If only I had accepted him with all his eccentricities and excesses. If only I had been an extraordinary rather than ordinary sister.

Of course death is so extraordinary it's hard to measure up. Many have heard the desperate wail, "You'll be sorry when I'm dead," from one whose love is not being served. It's a safe call. Of course we'll be sorry. There is no such thing as not being sorry when someone is dead. Even, or perhaps particularly, in the most fraught relationships.

We are sorry in more ways than they can imagine. As a forty-year-old friend of mine mourning her mother cried, "But I wasn't finished with her yet."

I wasn't finished with Bobby yet. There were questions that will now go unanswered. His life, like a poem, will be left to interpretation. Because of the geographical and emotional distance between us, I'd never had the long conversations with him as an adult that I have had with my sister. Conversations that ground us in childhood allowing us to get our bearings in adulthood. What was our family like for you? What was growing up like for you? How did you see us, our parents?

I try to forgive myself for not having those conversations. Now I begin to forgive him for not allowing them, although my grief had been fueled by rage at both George and Bobby for not letting me know that the end was near. For not giving me the opportunity for last words before it was too late. Death is the ultimate too late. It is now missed opportunity that I mourn along with the missing brother. Missed opportunity to love better.

I was eager for our planned September reunion because George, in telling of his love for Bobby, had restored my love in turn. We spoke for hours on the phone during Bobby's hospitalization. George sitting in his air-conditioned little house on a quiet Louisiana street and I with all my windows open to the muggy heat of Manhattan. I could never get warm that season. I wore socks by day and night. Cold dread had settled into my body.

George's great gift to me was that as we spoke, he took me back to a brother I had forgotten. He brought back Bobby's generous capacity for wonder and delight. "We have beautiful rose bushes in our backyard," he told me. "They are like our children, and sometimes Bobby comes running in to wake me up at six in the morning because another rose has bloomed and he wants me to come and see it. For him it is a celebration." Then he added, "Life is a celebration for Bobby."

He chose to celebrate without me, building walls that I could not cross. He made that choice rather than continuing to reach out only to feel his hand close on air. He took control of his loneliness by choosing it. My regret is that I didn't reach over the wall. It was too hard to scale, there were no chinks, no footholds, no encouraging shouts from the other side, "Just keep trying," so I gave up. Now am I beginning to learn that walls are built with only half a heart. The one who piles stone upon stone is longing for someone to stay his hand. But the mason wears a scowl. Sometimes he even hurls a rock as you approach. It takes courage and self-confidence to continue forward armorless and with extended hand.

I did not have that confidence, so retreated.

But now I know that if pain had reached out to pain, Bobby and I would have found similarity in sorrow. His would have been no stranger to my own. To be human is to be lost as well as found, to grieve as well as rejoice, and at times to feel inadequately loved even when loved. But we isolate ourselves in pain.

I try to remind myself that relationships among the living are two-sided. There were others who knew and, yes, loved Bobby better. I was important in his life, but not central. In forgiving myself, I have to accept that. There is a form of aggrandizement in remorse as though things would have been completely different if the mourner had done what had been left undone. The fact is that I might be suffering fewer regrets now if I had performed the "if onlys" then but they might have made no difference in our relationship.

Regret is a sad legacy. How different it would be if it had been my husband rather than my brother who had died. Having had an intense and passionate love affair for over twenty years, our love has taken on a life of its own. It continues to exist even when we take time out from it in times of stress or anger. It is there hovering waiting to be reclaimed. And it will continue to exist even when one lover is missing. Compared to that fire, regret is cold company.

The minister introduces us to an exercise "that has helped ease mourners' guilt." He instructs us, "Close your eyes and talk to the dead person. Express your regrets and then respond as you think the deceased might respond." Since the deceased is not in a position to forgive us, we are going to have to forgive ourselves. I try and a flood of remorse washes over me. As I want to stop it I know that I mustn't, that it has to wash over and away, like a river.

To live in remorse is to live backwards. If death is to have any meaning at all it is to teach us the power of love and to allow that power to propel us through the rest of our days.

So, I am grateful to George for the stepping stones to love that he tossed to me, skipping them across the sheer surface of water separating Manhattan from New Orleans.

A few weeks ago at Good Friday services, I heard, in a new way, the familiar story of Peter denying his knowledge of Jesus. No, he asserted, when he saw that to affirm his connection might cost him his life, no, I do not know this man, the Nazarene. For the first time I understood this denial as a failure of love. A forgiven failure, for foreseeing it, Jesus declared, "You are Peter, and on this rock I will build my church."

Today I wonder, will I be able to forgive myself as completely? Will I be able to become the rock on which I will build my life?

CHAPTER XI

"BLESSED ARE THEY WHO MOURN, FOR THEY SHALL BE COMFORTED"

"BLESSED ARE THEY WHO MOURN, FOR THEY SHALL BE COMFORTED"

I had long admired the poetry of the Beatitudes but had not understood their *sense* until I came to join my grief with others'. When I heard, "Blessed are the meek for they shall inherit the earth," I had thought, "Not my earth. Here the meek don't get a seat on the bus." And the pairing of "mourn" and "comfort" confused me.

In my family mourning was not done publicly. Therefore, I, as a child, assumed it was not done at all. Both sets of grandparents died and I recall hidden tears, the quick turn away to look out a window, the closing of a door. This mysterious behavior seemed to commence with the announcement of death and end immediately after the funeral.

Of course, if mourning is private, almost secretive as though shameful, there can be no comforting.

Now I discover that, if honest emotion is shared, the response tends to be compassionate, but if those who grieve don't bring up the subject of fatal illness and death, no one else will. Those who would comfort us are watching our eyes, awaiting our lead. No one can know how to help unless we teach them. Everyone is so unnerved by death that they feel inadequate to ease the pain of those it has robbed. Perhaps that explains letters, which at the time of Bobby's death failed to comfort, those that said, "Call if you need anything." "Let us know what we can do."

Now I understand that the correspondents were frightened and needed us to show them what to do, how to act. Needed us to let them know that they were safe, that our pain could not magically become theirs should we touch. That bad luck is not contagious. They could not know that no one in mourning will respond to cautious invitation. Mourners need the brave souls who dare to hold them, touch them, to stay rather than leave when the tears begin to flow. They do not need sage advice or perfect words. Simple human touch is the mourner's balm.

I always thought that those who grieved wanted to be left alone, because that's how it had been done in my family. Grief has become so removed from public places and collective consciousness, that it is as secretive as sex. Should we really be there to see it?

But grief is not a bedroom activity and must not be if we are to be comforted. The mourner cannot expect to make the calls, but the mourner can surrender to grief and not run and hide. And then the necessary hands will reach out to bolster and to hold.

Perhaps that is why the Grief Healing Group was an important companion on my journey through sorrow. It provided a safe place to cry, an atmosphere of quiet empathy. We expected nothing of ourselves, neither to comfort or be comforted, we were merely there with our grief. And we were not alone.

I was not a firsthand witness to death until I was forty-one years old. I had lived through an age that included the Vietnam War, starvation in Biafra and Ethiopia, the Pol Pot's slaughter of millions in Cambodia, the assassinations of Martin Luther King and John and Robert Kennedy, but I had never been in a room with death. When I was I lost my fear.

A friend of mine had taken her mother, Kathryn, a victim of Alzheimer's disease, into her home and cared for her for seven years. In the end Kathryn had forgotten how to swallow and seemed to be forgetting how to breathe. She died holding her daughter's hand.

I arrived twenty minutes later and joined my friend and her adult daughters in the bedroom where the body lay. One daughter held her grandmother's pale hand which, webbed with veins, looked like a porcelain road map. The other daughter sat at the base of the bed and rubbed her grandmother's tiny, size four, white foot. We spoke in whispers as though someone were sleeping. But we knew, in fact, no one was there.

At first I was shy about looking at the body. Would it be impolite to do so? An invasion of privacy? Everyone else was, but they were family. Were there any rules to be observed here? If so, no one had spelled them out, and so I looked, almost daring myself to do so, and as I did, began to understand how the concept of the spirit leaving the body might have been born. The corpse looked like a shell. A lovely, polished, empty shell.

A dead person does not look like a sleeping person. I am not certain how morticians create that illusion. Perhaps the folding of the hands, the makeup. But a dead person, untouched, looks like an unoccupied house.

As we sat in that room and talked and cried and at times reached out to touch the body, I was grateful that I could see that departure from this world had been as natural as entering it.

I was also grateful that in that room of loving friends we could make up the ritual of our mourning as we went along.

We held hands and stood around the foot of the bed. We said the Lord's Prayer. My friend then went to the head of the bed and kissed her mother's closed eyelids. "Good-bye, Darling," she said, and we left the room.

Then the death officials moved in. The police, the funeral parlor owner, the ambulance driver.

It helps me, when I recall my brother's last minutes, as relayed by George, to remember Kathryn and the evidence of her quiet, gentle departure.

I believe that Bobby's dying in George's arms eased his

way out of this life. He was not among strangers or attached to tubes. No alarm bells rang as he began his journey, no medical technicians rushed in to jam apparatus down his throat, to pound his retreating heart, to erect road blocks in the path of his departure. No one offended by death's power demanded, "One more day! One more month!" regardless of the quality of that day or month. Like Kathryn, he had the good fortune to die a dignified death, on his own terms, released from an undignified disease that had robbed him of all terms.

I have often wondered how the dying know when their time is drawing near. I have heard many stories of mothers who, fatally ill, hold on until Christmas night or the day after a child's birthday. I have one friend whose mother, ill with inoperable cancer, hung the wreaths and stockings, decorated the tree, made the roast beef and Yorkshire pudding, handed out the presents, and at eight P.M. after new dolls had been dressed and toy trucks driven and children bathed and tucked in for the night, said, "I think I'll go to the hospital now." She died at midnight.

Bobby must have known the true schedule of the rest of his life. After his death, George admitted this too. "I think he knew because when I returned home from St. John, I found notes from Bobby everywhere. In my sock drawer, under my mattress. And within a few days gifts that he'd ordered before we left began to arrive for me in the mail. He obviously knew that I'd be coming home alone."

Knew it and protected the rest of us from the knowledge. He was also protecting himself. He feared, George now tells me, that we would rush down to take control, and he wanted to control his own destiny. He was right. Once I knew that Bobby had AIDS, I tried to control even from a distance. Researching cures, calling to tell him of special Chinese herbs, of visualization, macrobiotic diets, garlic pills and evening primrose oil. I had no idea that the disease had progressed so far beyond my help.

CHAPTER XII
SIBLING GRIEF

SIBLING GRIEF

"Experiments indicate that the cues of kinship among tadpoles are more complex and numerous than had been previously believed."

Experiments indicate that even as far down the chain of life as the lowly tadpole there is bonding between siblings. Bonding against all odds. Tadpoles raised in isolation after hatching, when released into a pool of other tadpoles, swim to their siblings. "Even weeks later," according to an article in the Science section of the *Times*, "even if raised with unrelated tadpoles from the beginning."

So, I have no answer when strangers learning of my brother's death ask, "Were you close?" I am tempted, having recently learned about tadpoles, to answer, "Not in later years, but I'd swim to him in an instant."

I think of those tadpoles and wonder if rather than having been released to their siblings they had been kept apart, would they swim aimlessly, energized by yearning?

Were you close? Not in later years, but he's gone and so is a part of myself. Lately I've seen him in me, especially after long days of frustration. If I catch a glimpse of my face in a mirror I see his sad, blue eyes in my own. Throughout his life no matter how raucous he became, how loud his laughter, how merry his tale, his eyes remained mournful, as though part of a different face, a different person. The act went on without them.

I'd know him in a crowded pool even if we'd been separated since birth. By our eyes we would know each other.

There have been studies of twins separated and raised by different families, sometimes continents apart. When the research teams tracked them down they discovered that each of a pair was a mechanic with a passion for chess. Or both played the bassoon and worked in banks and married girls named Darlene.

"Amazing!" we said as we read this. "Just amazing!" There goes the old nature vs. nurture dialogue, we thought. Nature raises its hand from the back of the room and when finally called upon, inevitably has the right answer.

The grief of siblings is often overlooked. "People keep asking me how my mother is," I was told by a friend whose brother is dying. "Sometimes I want to cry, 'What about me? Doesn't anybody wonder how I'm feeling?'"

In response to her book, *Shrapnel in the Heart,* Laura Palmer received a letter from a woman whose brother, a Vietnam War veteran, died of a drug overdose. The writer mentioned a book she had been reading about the grief of the wives, parents and children of Vietnam casualties. Siblings, she wrote, were not considered. "As though the war was fought by only children." She continued, "I was alienated from my brother while he drank. He became violent when he drank. And he drank or smoked dope almost all the time." Thus her mother "was astonished that I took a midnight flight from California to the East Coast as soon as I learned that Bill was dying. She assumed I wouldn't care, couldn't forgive . . .

"I loved my brother with all my heart. My heart just wasn't big enough to hold him and me and the pain of what life and the Vietnam War had handed him.

"I feel very alone with my grief . . . When my brother died, most of my friends barely even knew I *had* a brother. I had been so silent about him."

Siblings may be ambivalent about their relationships in life, but in death the power of their bond strangles the surviving heart. Death reminds us that we are part of the same river, the same flow from the same source, rushing toward the same destiny.

Were you close? Yes, but we didn't know it then.

The family that survives the death of a child and sibling will not do so without first falling into chaos. Lately ecological theorists are citing the work of Steve Packard, science director of the Illinois Conservancy, whose work, according to *The New York Times*, supports "the contention that ecosystems assemble and develop not haphazardly, as if by accident, but in special patterns and sequences, according to specific affinities. If even a few key species are missing . . . the ecosystem will not function." A family is an ecosystem.

And, considering the hot passion beneath the more or less ordered familial form, it is no wonder that things fall apart when the formation disintegrates. No wonder funerals are the frequent favored settings for novelists and playwrights. This is where grief rips off the veil of familial politesse and reveals primitive, raw, unguarded emotion. If you threw a can of gasoline into the center of the grieving family circle, you wouldn't need a match to set it aflame.

Death says, "All rules are off." The death of a sibling ignores the natural order of progression. Do not underestimate the rage in mourning. You can't fight it out with God or the deceased, so you thrash it out with your world. The family that survives will do so only after a bloody civil war. And then, if all goes well, the armiies will lie down and surrender.

In my family the war broke out between my beloved sister and myself. Irony this blatant would never play off-Broadway, but it played itself out in our lives. Where we had always reached for one another to share life's experiences, we now threw punches. Where once we had understood each other, we now seemed to speak different languages. I loved her but she could not feel it. She loved me, but all I could sense was her anger. I ran from it, knowing full well that retreat was what I most regretted in my relationship with Bobby.

There was nothing our parents could do to mend the rift. They saw the madness in our tossing each other to the winds when fate had done that to our brother. They encouraged phone calls and visits, they delivered messages of consolation, all to no avail. Now I wonder if Becky and I were taking turns acting out the role of fate. Were we playing the God game? Were we shaking our fists at the heavens and shouting, "We can do it too. We aren't helpless. We can make our beloveds disappear from our lives." Were we identifying with the aggressor, that age-old ploy of the weak, the helpless and the broken? What happens when the aggressor is God? We bring ruin, of proportions we had never dreamed of, down upon our heads.

It started so simply. In the chaos that followed Bobby's death, my daughter Rebecca temporarily broke up with her fiancée Chuck, a young man loved by all family members. In September Becky called me to express grave concern about Rebecca's new boyfriend. I responded that this was Rebecca's business and that I would stand by her choices.

In a family where disagreement is rarely expressed, this was experienced by both of us as the opening of a large chasm, as though to disagree was to betray. We began to find it more and more difficult to speak to one another. Soon there was silence. And I thought of her every hour of every day.

Many years ago our father told us that the reason we family members were not allowed to fight with each other was that he did not see anger as part of a loving relationship. Now that I too am a parent, I understand that this belief came from his desire to create for his children an environment free of the familiar pain of his own childhood. It is often the only guide we have in our all consuming drive to save our children from harm.

Death is the ultimate regressor and I clung to these earliest lessons as I was tossed back into childhood. I knew that if Becky and I were angry, we must not love each other.

She accused me of being cold, remote, unresponsive. I told her that I didn't want any more pain in my life. She took this to mean that I didn't want her in my life. What did I mean? Pain wasn't something in my life, it was my life and it was exacerbated by her absence, not her presence. Pain was the rack on which I hung my clothes.

There is no answer to what I meant or why I acted as I did. Grief eats reason for breakfast. There is probably good sense in the admonition to widows: Don't do anything for one year following bereavement! Don't move! Don't marry! Don't change jobs! Don't sleep with strangers! In other words, during that initial year of loss you are not, as my grandmother's generation would say, "in your right mind."

I kept wondering, how can my sister hate me? After all, I taught her to walk! I thought it and believed it exactly as I had when I was five years old and held her hand as she took her first steps. I believed then that without me she never would have learned. Thirty-nine years later I was believing it with the same certainty, convinced that she owed me loyalty because of my single act of heroism.

Of course, as young children we know perfectly well that we are life savers. We know the dark secret that but for our control, but for turning resentment into nervous guardianship, our younger siblings would have been drowned or smothered at our hands.

I taught her to walk! I spared her life! How can she turn on me? At the time these seemed like perfectly reasonable considerations.

I have heard similar stories. A friend's sister has not spoken to him "for twenty years, ever since our mother died. She blames me." For what? "I don't know. Her death, I suppose." My sister and I were more fortunate. Our love survived the war and we, hobbling veterans, are helping each other walk again. A few baby steps at a time. It takes a long time to rebuild a family. There is no Marshall Plan for mourners.

CHAPTER XIII

JUNE:
SUFFERING ISN'T
FOUND IN
LEDGER BOOKS

JUNE: SUFFERING ISN'T FOUND IN LEDGER BOOKS

"Out of whose womb comes the ice?" Out of whose womb comes death? The same womb that gave us life. Is death the price we pay for the gift of life?

Do I consider it a price too high? Will the high cost of loving make me a spendthrift lover? From now on will I live cautiously, always holding something back, so that I can afford to pay the price?

Today, as I rushed up Madison Avenue from 72nd to 79th Street, I glanced at gallery windows without slowing my pace. Renoir, Dubuffet, Utrillo, Benton, all a blur, like a landscape outside the windows of a speeding car, untouched and unexperienced. Curiosity, at a point, caused me to glance sideways, but I then hurried on, refusing to be engaged. Showers of color sped by untouched by my heart or eye.

When my sister was three years old and I seven, our family drove from Connecticut to California. Or that's what our parents told us at the time. My sister, on the other hand, was convinced that our car never left the driveway of our home and that the passing landscape was a movie our parents were running outside the car windows. Great kidders, our parents.

If we pretend it's all a movie, do we have to make the trip? If we only catch a glimpse of life out of the corner of our eye, do we still have to pay the full price of admission? We're paying it every day, the only choice we have is whether to rent or own our lives.

I consider my brother's death at such a young age a price too high to pay and so lately I've refused, on occasion, to stop and stare and absorb life's brush strokes and vibrant colors.

Not too many years ago, I dreamed that a beloved old beau who died at twenty-one returned to earth and was walking through the snow outside my childhood home. Amazed and euphoric, I ran out to greet him, crying, "But I thought you were dead!" He merely laughed and we embraced. I pray that I don't have that dream about my brother, for the price of waking is too dear.

On the other hand, if we all have to pay at the exit gate, we might as well get our money's worth before we leave. From everything I learn from his friends, Bobby did just that. He lived at 78 r.p.m.s as though he knew his was not a long-playing record. He had to get his song out *fast*.

To my mind he drank too much, smoked too much, slept around too much, spent too much money. Now I wonder, why did I consider it any of my business? Why hadn't I made it my business to simply love him? Even as he lay in the hospital, my sister and I were plotting his future course. He'd have to clean up his act, we insisted to each other, making hospital corners of the loose ends of his life. I was furious at him "for letting this happen to himself." She responded quietly, "He may not have behaved admirably, but his behavior doesn't warrant a death sentence." She was right of course. Something wasn't adding up.

Disease as metaphor is as common as it is ancient. Job's friend Eliphaz explains to Job, the most honorable of men, that he must have done some terrible wrong in order to "deserve" his suffering. "'Think now, who that was innocent ever perished? Or where were the upright cut off?'"

Such thinking was apparent in a letter to the editors of *The*

New York Times Magazine in response to an article I wrote about Bobby's death. Richard A. Young, a partner in a Manhattan law firm and a modern-day Eliphaz took me to task for my gratitude that Bobby had found love in this world, even if that love was with another man. "Apparently, she means that even if it kills her brother."

It was a familiar response. One that was more common in the early days of AIDS. The redneck, "They-got-what-they-had-comin'-to-'em" belief. It's just another way of trying to make order out of chaos. A balance in an unbalanced universe. Design in a world that is random. Poetry is one attempt, primitive belief another.

Death is neither punishment nor a price we pay. It doesn't all add up in the end. It doesn't follow the patterns of justice or capitalism. We bring this context to death, but it eludes our plots, our plans, our attempts to categorize. Beyond the medical definitions that have to do with cessation of brain and heart function lies the great mystery.

Too often, mysteries make us mad. We insist on answers. It's positively un-American to say, "I don't know." But death says, no, there are mysteries to be accepted, not answered. More and more I am drawing comfort from that and finding that as I come to the limits of my knowledge, I am approaching the limitlessness of my heart.

CHAPTER XIV
OF WHAT USE RELIGION?

OF WHAT USE RELIGION?

If there is a God, a beneficent God, why is suffering part of human experience? In the aftermath of the holocaust, there are few thoughtful "believers" who are not stumped. Why should I trust in a merciful God who would allow hundreds of thousands of little children to be slaughtered? If God is senseless, then what kind of God is that? If there is a God, why are we allowed to be stirred to greed over and over, inspired to kill one another?

In *A Grief Observed,* C. S. Lewis seems to think that to God's ears, such pondering may be nonsense:

> *Can a mortal ask questions which God finds unanswerable? Quite easily, I should think. All nonsense questions are unanswerable. How many hours are there in a mile? Is yellow square or round? Probably half the questions we ask—half our great theological and metaphysical problems—are like that.*

I can no longer tolerate a romantic, childhood notion of God but have, in the midst of great distress, sensed a presence of strength and clarity, a guiding hand as I sailed beyond the edge of the map, beyond the edge of my known world, beyond the threshold where it is warned, "Here be dragons." In the months of Bobby's illness there were times when I came to prayer because it was all I had. Life had let me down.

Medicine had let me down. As I closed my eyes and retreated from the world, I felt that I was alone in a cold, dark dungeon, but slowly, over time, I began to notice that in that darkness there seemed to be a door under which there was a slim ray of light, not warm, or burning or luminous. It was like a clear intelligence. Steady and unwavering, it neither astounded nor blinded. It quite simply showed me a way and closed out all other thoughts. It was here in this place within myself, this dark, silent, revealing place that while praying I learned to pray.

Prayer had been part of my life since I was a young child. Grace before meals and bony knees against hard floors at bedtime. "If I should die before I wake . . ." Prayers against imagined dangers. Prayers for favors. Deal-making prayers. "Dear God, if you make my mom let me spend the night at Linda's, I'll never be bad again." Slowly I learned the poetry and dignity of prayer through the ritual of the Episcopal service.

But before Bobby's illness I had not known a truly felt prayer, one in which the one who prays and the one beseeched join as guide and guided. One day as I prayed, the course of the prayer changed. "God, don't let him die!" became, "God, help me to love him well in the time that is left." It was as though I had been lifted in arms and turned around in a different direction. I had not changed the prayer, it was changed for me.

We learn surprisingly little from our profound experiences. I have not prayed as deeply since. Nor do I wish to, for the land of my soul was the land of my dread.

Although devout as a child, I took time out in the '70s when Jesus started appearing on bumper stickers, T-shirts and on the poster on my brother's bedroom wall. For a time I would not claim Christianity, which seemed to have become the exclusive province of closed-minded groupies "born again" and seeing a light that caused their eyes to glaze over. And there were others, who coming drugged from the '60s found that getting high on Jesus was a pretty "good trip." I knew too many people who were turning their backs on those whom they did not consider "good Christians," when I fervently believed and continue to that not one of us is in a position to judge that. Too many Jesus bumper stickers were on pickup trucks equipped with gun racks. Too little of being "born again" had to do with charity.

Too many "good Christians" were talking about burning books and saving fetuses for whom they were unwilling to provide a safe world. If Jesus was "theirs," he most certainly wasn't mine.

It made no difference that Jesus was also Paul Tillich's and Reinhold Niebuhr's and Pierre Teilhard de Chardin's and C. S. Lewis's and William James's and Martin Luther King's. My mind was as tightly closed as those whose brand of Christianity I abhorred.

In the '80s I began to search, half-heartedly, for a church in Manhattan and finally settled into Riverside, feeling at home and uplifted in a congregation that was comprised of scruffy college kids, middle-class suburbanites, blacks, and riffraff like me. Each Sunday as I walked down that aisle I felt that my soul was coming unzipped, that I was vulnerable and exposed. Anything could happen. It frightened me enough that I only attended sporadically.

And then, at forty, I decided to join a church, throwing my lot in with the others there who came to connect with possibility. The possibility of answers and the bigger possibilities of hope and redemption. I suppose that it was age appropriate to look for "a spiritual home." I no longer wanted to be an observer, as I was at Riverside. I wanted to belong. I wanted a place where it was safe to be me and it was safe to cry and where I might learn something of the mysteries of faith and prayer. I went to visit a neighborhood church where the minister informed me, "We have a lot of folks your age joining. Especially the yuppies. They get to be forty and realize something's missing from their lives. In spite of kids and cars and country houses and co-ops and spouses ... something's missing."

I suppose that they, as I, were experiencing an amorphous yearning. I wanted to connect without knowing the object of my connection. I was homesick but didn't know the way home. I was fortunate to find this church, "Just in the nick of time," as a friend observed. For it was soon after I joined that Bobby became ill, and it was there that I was safe to experience the full, crushing weight of my grief.

The first Sunday in September after the summer away and the first visit back to church since Bobby's death, I sobbed through the hymns, the prayer, the sermon. Anonymous hands passed Kleenex down the pews and even as I cried, I was thinking, "I had no idea that I felt this awful. I had thought that all the tears had been shed." I had come home, to the place where it is safe to feel terrible.

In December, seventeen months after Bobby's death, my (and his) niece and nephew walked the aisle of that same church as flower girl and ring bearer in my daughter's wedding. The unexpected extent of my joy was as mysterious as the extent of my grief, and as powerful a transport out of time and space. They seemed to rise together and mingle there below the Georgian ceiling until grief dissipated and a shower of exuberance fell upon me.

My joy connected me to all joy that had ever come before, as my grief had bound me to all sorrow remembered. Perhaps religion serves to guide us through the labyrinths of pain and confusion to this spiritual plane of resurrected passion. Perhaps that's the most we can ask of it. And perhaps that is enough.

CHAPTER XV

JULY:
ANNIVERSARIES

JULY: ANNIVERSARIES

My husband and I tiptoe around the edges of this day in late May. I have avoided looking at the calendar for a week. A year ago today we learned of Bobby's hospitalization, now we begin the countdown to July 21, the first anniversary of his death. We're alert. We're edgy. We're mystified. Two days ago Bob said, "Something seems amiss. The way you feel the day after an especially bad dream. Just a sense that things aren't right."

Yesterday morning I awakened with fear in my heart. I couldn't pin it down for analysis and dissection. Free floating fear. I finally determined that it had something to do with the calendar. "I'm so anxious because I have so many appointments today," I told my husband. "How will I ever accomplish everything? There's too much to do and too little time."

It was only this morning as we awakened and reached for each other holding tight as though adrift on a life raft that we accepted again, as we have had to hundreds of times before, that there are situations in which determined intellect cannot conquer primitive instinct. Anniversaries demand our attention. The soul has its own clock, its own calendar and the teeth of our souls were chattering with remembered terror.

One year after the 1989 earthquake in San Francisco, *The New York Times* ran an article entitled, "A Year Later, Bay Area Jumps at Tiny Rattles." Those who lived through it report that they are particularly alert and fearful on October 13, the anniversary of the quake. "There's a trigger-quick readiness to think something terrible is about to happen again," said Jane Burka. Robert Maynard observed, "I am never unmindful of the fact that in one split second this terrible thing can happen. Every lovely moment can suddenly be visited by that specter. There is no unremitting joy now because there's always the other side."

The other side is with us through the rest of May, through June and into mid-July when we leave Manhattan and go to our boat, as we did last year at this time. At anchor in a quiet New England harbor, I am unnerved by a growing sense of doom and attribute it to the weather. Hot and hazy, "Less than one mile visibility in fog and occasional drizzle," the marine weather tape replays the same message day after day. July 14, 15, 16, 17. We're getting closer and closer to the twenty-first and I become certain that something terrible is going to happen until slowly I begin to realize that no, it already did.

We sail to my parents' island to be with them for the night of the twentieth and the following day. We are ignorant in many ways, but this much we know, we must be together. On the morning of the twenty-first I row ashore to take a solitary walk on the beach where we used to play as children. The fog is so heavy it seems to flatten and slick the waves that roll to the beach, fold and recede without breaking. It's a morning without sound until a single goldfinch atop a choke-cherry tree begins to sing, splitting the silence with the shock of its high trill. "Heaven can't be better than this," I think. Heaven can't be better than a sudden flash of feathered gold relieving gray. Of perfect pitch challenging silence. Wherever Bobby is, he is deprived of this, and I weep for him anew.

This land and seascape summon and bind us across the years to friends and family who gather here summer after summer. Like these waves, year follows year in smooth succession with each seeming much like the one that preceded it. So little changes that those of us in our twenties, thirties, and forties continue to think of ourselves and each other as "the children," and probably will until our parents and grandparents die, forcing us by their absence to change our collective perception. The "grown-ups" are those who were adult when we were children in fact.

This island makes us believe in order and stability. It's not unusual, on a sunny day, to meet four generations of a family enjoying a picnic on the beach. The children of our playmates now play with our children. We who benefited years ago from the kindness of the "grown-ups" return the favor and teach what we were taught—the games of capture the flag and blind man's bluff, how to make the perfect drip sand castle, how to row, sail, swim. Today could be a day when Bobby, Becky and I were children. We could have believed it would last forever.

But last summer changed all that. These families that we had known all our lives and adopted as our own, wh if unrelated by genes were claimed by name, Aunt Kitsy and Uncle Wye, Aunt Smoke and Uncle Dave, gathered among the bayberry, beach heather and cherry trees to recall and say goodbye to Bobby. By all rights he should have been standing there. Time had been set on its head.

Everything that day was familiar and totally changed. The sun glittered on the pale hair of babies and their parents. I kept thinking of Wallace Stevens's lines, "The hair of my blond/ Is dazzling,/As the spittle of cows threading the wind." There was cow spittle everywhere and I sought distance and safety in the poem.

Barefooted toddlers meandered in and out of the folds of their mothers' billowing cotton skirts, or came to rest between their fathers' legs, or sat on the grass and sucked their thumbs. Everyone wore the "dress-up" clothes stuffed away in the backs of closets, untouched year after year until there is an occasion that would call for a flowered skirt, a pair of faded red trousers. From a distance the scene could have been mistaken for a meadow of wild flowers, soft reds and pastels, planted in green, swaying in the wind.

But up close, everyone bore the disoriented expression of children awakened from a bad dream. We were all wondering, "Where are we?" in this place that had always reassured us as to exactly who and where we were.

The wind blew up from the harbor and sent the sides of a red tablecloth dancing like a banner around the picnic table bearing familiar cocktail fare—potato chips surrounding a bowl of sour cream and onion-soup-mix dip. Our version of Proust's madeleines.

Friends spoke to me and it was exhausting to respond in turn. I wished them well, I was heartened that they had come, but I could not make my brain and voice connect. I tried to keep my lips from quivering long enough to hold a steady smile, to mimic those who smiled at me.

When all had gathered, the "dean" of the community, the man whose family had been coming here the longest, the man who had taught us as six-year-olds how to dig steamers in the morning, clean and serve them up for lunch, who had started the first sailing classes that became our "yacht club," who now taught our children and grandchildren how to build wooden boats, officially "welcomed" us. He tried to be his affable self, the self with which we were familiar. But this was unfamiliar territory. He looked at his feet. He looked up at the white clouds blowing across the sky. He looked out at us and the kindness of his blue eyes held unfamiliar pain. We were here to say good-bye to one of the children. Nothing had prepared us for that.

When it was my husband's turn to speak we could barely hear him above the rustle of leaves and the slapping of halyards in the harbor. "The loss of a loved family member never seems timely, but Bobby was our loved child and younger brother." He caught his breath and continued, "My generation accepts death as the inevitable, in the usual order of things somehow. Reasonable people struggle to make order . . . to help make it better for each other and our children. As Dotsy said to Barbie when Bobby was sick, 'I can't help feeling I want to kiss it to make it better.' Bobby's death seems our total failure."

Up until now, we had been fortunate in our misfortunes. Our kisses could often make it better. AIDS destroyed that conceit.

My brother-in-law, Dan, took his place before the crowd

and searched for "the kindest face" he could find to fix his eyes upon. He found a young friend with whom Becky had shared her childhood and who now stood with his daughter at his side and six-year-old son on his shoulders. The wind blew the notes Dan held in his shaking hand as he squinted against the sun and tears. "Becky, our kids, John and Lydia, and I were traveling in California when Bobby died," he began. "When John and Lydia woke up that unhappy morning, Becky told them the sorrowful news. John, who is eight, unleashed a mourner's wail, a wrenching, extended sob as natural as breath itself—he'd never seen anyone else mourn. His pain was natural, and it was deep. 'It's not fair,' he exclaimed.

"It was the wisdom of innocence. John saw the unfairness we all see—our being untimely robbed of those things that define what we know as 'Bobbyness': his playfulness, his humor, his signature pleasure in nearly everything found around him. It was as if he were part of some anthropomorphic solar system; most of the time, in fact, Bobby was the very sun at its center."

He recalled one of the newspaper columns Bobby had written after one of the "grown-ups" had died. Bobby shared memories of his friend with the readers and then at the end of the piece, he addressed our parents. "I will cling to these memories, and perhaps we will relive them together as we recall that which is irrevocably ours." Dan returned the words to Bobby as he said, "Robert Allen Lazear, Jr., was—and is, and will be—irrevocably ours."

He then walked to my sister who put her arms around him as his shoulders sank and his sobs came as his son's had, "as natural as breath itself."

It was over. People mingled around the lawn. Kindhearted people who had made it possible for me to grow up with an unwavering belief in goodness. People who had taken turns parenting us. Whose kindness became our model when it was our turn to be the parents. Their presence was a reminder of a reality from which we'd been tossed as though off the edge of the earth, as though gravity had forgotten us.

No one ate much nor did they have the heart for drink. They hugged us. They moved on, out through the garden, through the field, across the beach and home again.

I follow the same path this morning, walking up from the beach and down to the edge of the lawn in front of my parents' house. There is a bench under the chokecherry tree where Bobby's ashes are buried. It sits high on a bluff, providing a view out over the harbor and far across Vineyard Sound to the ocher, red and gray cliffs of Gay Head on Martha's Vineyard.

The Greeks had their sacred groves. We now have this shaded realm. Sitting here in the silence, nothing seems to exist but the breeze on my skin, the scent of brine and sense of Bobby. The Bobby Dan described. The sadder Bobby I have recalled. The kind Bobby who understood that I would need this place.

Last year I sat here as our friends departed and Bob held me in his arms offering me the only comfort I could accept, his own sorrow and his own strength. We watched the boats in the harbor and I thought again of Brueghel's painting, *Landscape with the Fall of Icarus*. The sailors navigating below were ignorant of the disaster that had befallen us, were oblivious to the boy who had plummeted from the sky, his "white legs disappearing into the green water."

As we sat in silence, a kite suddenly rose up from behind the bluff in front of us. It hovered for a moment within four feet of our faces and then swooped back and straight up to the top of the chokecherry tree. We followed its course, amused by the loud flapping of its fabric as it perched lightly on the edges of the branches. Its hues were garish, clashing, vibrant. Oranges, reds, yellows, purples, all in shades deeper, louder, truer than our eyes were accustomed to. After it had captured our full attention, it lifted again, more bird than kite, and fluttered for a moment above the tree before seeming to bow in a form of farewell.

It was then that we noticed that it had no string. It was completely unattached to anything. We had imagined a small child's hand on the beach below. A small child clinging to a ball of string, looking up and gasping as the kite lit upon the tree. But no. There was no string, no child, nothing at the other end of the wild display.

It drifted, about ten feet off the ground, over the lawn, the roof of the house and the garden. It floated above the meadow to the edge of the orchard where it faded out of sight, as a puff of smoke is lost when it merges with air.

I looked at my father who had been standing at the garden gate and staring up at the kite. When he caught my gaze from across the lawn, he smiled and shrugged.

Bob and I looked at each other and whispered simultaneously, "Bobby! That was Bobby!" And we laughed until we cried. And then, holding tightly to one another, cried until we laughed again.

CHAPTER XVI

SAFE RETURN

To arrive where you are,
to get from where you are not,
you must go by a way
wherein there is no ecstasy—T. S. Eliot

SAFE RETURN

When you finally walk into the light, its brightness doesn't require that you hide your eyes. There is no trumpet's blare from which to protect your ears. You make the bed as usual, pour coffee, read the morning paper, walk the dog, and go about daily life. And you do the same again and again. It is only after a few days, or has it been weeks, that you realize you are walking a little lighter. You hear yourself laughing and make note of it. You are looking forward to something a few months ahead. You aren't watching your back.

Emerging from grief is not as dramatic as birth or home-coming. When you were deep within grief's tempest, you dreamed of safe return and imagined a hero's welcome and Athena holding back the dawn. But this has been a private journey and at its end there are no welcoming committees, no ticker-tape parades. Most people didn't even know you were gone, and it took a while for you to notice that you'd returned. It's not even apparent to the naked eye that you have changed since departure, although you have.

You were there when the bowels of the earth rumbled and growled with a great colliding of boulder and stone. Your foundations shifted and threatened to open into nothingness. It had seemed that the world as you knew it was coming to an end. And in some ways, it did. A survivor of the San Francisco earthquake reported, "This place has changed its idea of itself." So have you.

After Ernest Shackleton trekked over mountains of snow and ice to safety and after a rescue party was launched to retrieve his men, others tried to follow in his footsteps. But no one has ever been able to duplicate his march. That he did it is a miracle, most say. Impossible, say others.

It's no different from the journey through grief which we all take sooner or later, ill-equipped as we are we set out over merciless terrain to save ourselves. To stay behind on the ice means that we will go numb and sleep and eventually die, and there are times when that seems a preferable alternative to crossing the vast, empty, uncharted fields of snow.

No journey duplicates another, so we who have been there fail to tell those who follow how to get from the point of embarkation to the point of return. I try to retrace my steps, but can no longer find my footsteps. The snow begins to fill them. The landscape begins to blur.